SPINDLE
TURNING

The best from **WOODTURNING** *magazine*

SPINDLE TURNING

The best from **WOODTURNING** *magazine*

GUILD OF MASTER CRAFTSMAN PUBLICATIONS LTD

This collection first published in 1996 by
GUILD OF MASTER CRAFTSMAN PUBLICATIONS LTD,
Castle Place, 166 High Street, Lewes,
East Sussex BN7 1XU

© GMC Publications Ltd 1996

ISBN 1 86108 016 6

Printed and bound in Great Britain by
the University Press, Cambridge

Cover photographs supplied by Dave Regester

CONTENTS

NOTES

PLEASE NOTE that names, addresses, prices etc. were correct at the time the articles were originally published, but may since have changed.

MEASUREMENTS
Cautionary Note

THROUGHOUT the book instances will be found where a metric measurement has fractionally varying imperial equivalents, usually within $1/16$ in either way. This is because in each particular case the closest imperial equivalent has been given. For this reason it is recommended, particularly on the smaller projects, that a drawing is made of the work to ensure that the measurements have not lost anything in translation.

Also, although the measurements given here are carefully calculated and are accurate, some variation may occur when pieces are hand turned, so care must be taken and adjustment may be necessary as the work progresses.

A mixture of metric and imperial measurements should NEVER be used – always use either one or the other.

ℰℐℰ

INTRODUCTION

WOODTURNING magazine has reported on all types of turning since its launch in 1990. Between-centres or spindle turning has always been a feature, often overshadowed by more spectacular styles of bowl turning.

Turning between centres is the original form of the craft, dating back millennia. Before the invention of faceplates and chucks, even bowls were turned between centres. The core pieces from bowls turned on pole-lathes have been found on many archaeological digs.

Spindle work is now the most frequently seen form of turning. In most homes it is present more as component parts for furniture than complete turned items. The turning of components involves accuracy and work off the lathe, which may explain why spindle work is sometimes regarded as less glamorous than bowl turning.

A bowl can be completed on the lathe, but a chair leg is just a shaped piece of wood until it is joined to the rest of the parts. The joints require precision and it is usual for the legs to match – repetition work also demands accuracy.

This book is compiled from issues of *Woodturning* published from 1990 to the beginning of 1996, and covers a range of projects and technical articles. There are features on turning components such as chair legs, repetition turning, complete projects and technical pieces on how to get the best from tools and equipment.

The aims of this book are to allow those new to *Woodturning* magazine to see the best of what has already been published and to draw together articles for those turners whose main interest is spindle turning. It also gives long-time readers a chance to replace articles they may have lost, as some back issues of *Woodturning* have sold out.

Neil Bell,
Editor, *Woodturning*

Ernie Conover is our contributing editor in America. He teaches woodworking in general, and woodturning in particular, at Conover Workshops, a school he and his wife Susan operate together. In addition to writing and lecturing widely, he is a technical consultant to a number of companies on design and manufacture of woodworking tools and machines.

In Quest of the Perfect Handle

ERNIE CONOVER

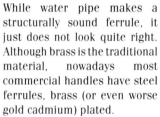

Turning a handle for your favourite gouge is a dandy spindle turning project that will put an individual signature on a tool, making it yours and yours alone.

The most overlooked and obvious project is turning a tool handle. Few turners turn their own handles, however, and the reason escapes me. In fact I find it a complete enigma. 'Handled' turning tools dominate the market — I am told they account for 90 per cent. Is this a matter of 'not being able to see the forest for the trees?' I have even wondered (in my most sinister thoughts) if the reason might be because turners might really have to see, every day, that it is difficult to turn two things exactly alike. Also they would have to really live with the fruits of their labour.

Well, it is confession time. All but one or two of my tools have personally turned handles, and no two are exactly alike — only nearly alike. The differences help me to sort out one tool from another when in a jumbled pile on the bench. And that, my friend, is a definite gain! I prescribe turning new handles for your tools, and buying unhandled tools (if you can still find any), in the future —turner heal yourself!

tool, making it yours and yours alone. With a bit of thought and experimentation, you can even devise an ergonomic design that makes turning intuitive. A handle that you turn yourself is so superior to the kind you receive on the average tool. I recommend pitching the factory variety in the wood stove and replacing them. Remember, a manufacturer is only giving you a handle because 90 per cent of the market demands it.

Ferrules

The reason I hear most often given as an excuse not to turn a handle is that a suitable ferrule cannot be found. This is balderdash, as any number of common items can be made into ferrules.

The Classic, a perfect blend of form and function!

While water pipe makes a structurally sound ferrule, it just does not look quite right. Although brass is the traditional material, nowadays most commercial handles have steel ferrules, brass (or even worse gold cadmium) plated.

Being a traditionalist, I prefer brass. So I buy brass tubing from an industrial supplier of the product. I also keep a sharp lookout for the odd scrap of brass that will be suitable for my purposes. I have often found discarded lengths of brass tubing that yielded splendid ferrules. Also do not overlook large cartridge cases — it is fun to beat swords into ploughshares. Another great source is old bronze bearings. Although they look about half-way between brass and copper, they do the job and they are cheap. I buy them surplus for $.05 each.

Finally using brass wire to wrap the handle, forming a ferrule, works great. A small brass brad to tie the wire off to helps. Drive the brad near the end of the tenon and tie off to it. Now start winding at the shoulder, passing over the starting end. As you

The fact is, turning a handle for your favourite gouge is a dandy spindle turning project that will put an individual signature on a

Many people in the U.S. use 12mm ½" or 20mm ¾" copper water pipe. The size given is the inside diameter of the pipe.

approach the brad, clip the starting end off and now wind up to the brad and tie off again. Clip the excess and drive the brad flush.

Since most woodworkers cut their ferrules with a hacksaw, the ends will be left rough and out of square. This is easily fixed with the lathe. Brass will scrape very well as it enjoys negative rake. In a metalworking lathe a brass tool is ground to a 5° negative rake angle. For us woodturners, we simply point the scraper downhill as we are used to and we will get spendid results. Turn a hardwood mandrel with a shoulder and tap the freshly hacksawed blank onto it. Now face the end with a scraper and reverse the blank on the mandrel. Tap it back so that the freshly faced end seats on the shoulder. Face the second end and polish with 000 steel wool. Be careful only to use a very small bit of steel wool as it can be wound up in the lathe. A big piece will take your fingers with it while a small piece will only confound itself. Now polish with polishing compound or rouge.

Tapered Mandrel for Facing Ferrule

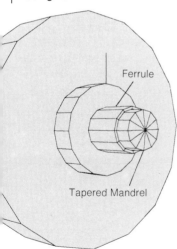

Ferrule

Tapered Mandrel

Fitting

Fitting the ferrule is something that gives many people fits, but it is quite simple. The easiest way to do the job is with a special dead centre in the tailstock. It is a variety described by Frank Pain in his delightful book *The Practical Woodturner*.

Although not commercially available, it is easy to cobble up yourself and makes ferrule fitting a breeze. Essentially it is just a cup centre with an extended body. The ferrule is slipped over the body before work is mounted and is ever ready for reference during the turning process. In fact the lathe need not even be stopped except in the final stages of fitting.

Extended Cup Centre makes fitting ferrules a breeze

The scrap bin at a machine tool supply store will usually yield a Morse taper something or other that can be modified to make it an extended centre. It is better if it is not hardened, so I always take a file along on foraging expeditions so that I can check this. Although a cup centre is better, a 60° point is fine and this can be made by filing while the taper is under power in the headstock of your wood lathe.

A ferrule should be a press fit with a good amount of interference between it and the tenon. Three things will help with getting the ferrule to fit properly. The first is to lightly chamfer the leading edge so that the ferrule can get an easy start. The second is to very slightly taper the first one quarter of the tenon. This will allow you to get the ferrule on the tenon far enough to align it with the axis and not have it cocked to one side. Finally a small groove or undercut at the base of the shoulder, coupled with undercutting the actual shoulder, will help in two ways.

It allows the ferrule to come square and flush to the shoulder with no air gaps, and it is a place for debris to collect if some of the wood is planed away by the ferrule as it seats itself.

Design

Actual design of a handle is quite arbitrary, and almost anything goes. The main thing is to have something comfortable without it being too phallic — a definite tendency by many beginners. If in doubt, look at some old tools in a flea market or museum. The Victorians made splendid handles that exemplified a marriage between form and function. If Bauhaus is more to your liking, that is fine too, in fact anything goes.

A couple of things to remember though. I like a handle to have some definite points that I can feel as I change grips further back for increased leverage. This can be anything from a cove or bead to a slight swelling. Additionally the handle should have sufficient diameter to give you a comfortable grip. Much of the control of a tool is in the grip and sufficient diameter gives both a relaxed grip and additional frictional area. Overly small diameters are tiring and exacerbate white knuckle syndrome, the affliction of new turners.

So called 'long and strong' handles on commercial tools today, are neither long nor strong. A long and strong handle should be at least 460mm 18″ and have a grip at the butt end resembling a

cricket or baseball bat. Since 90 per cent of the control of a bowl gouge is radial and accomplished with the right hand, a good diameter at the butt is most vital. Spindle turning tools need a handle from 125mm 5″ to 305mm 12″ long depending on the tool and its intended purpose.

Wood

Choice of wood for a handle is important. It should be a straight-grained variety, free of knots and with good tangential/radial strength. It should not be too heavy, but not too light. Elm, ash hickory, maple and sycamore are excellent.

Beech is OK, especially European beech which is quite different from American beech. They are both the same genus but different species. While the European is delightful, the American is rather cantankerous. It is difficult to dry and not terribly stable.

Boxwood is wonderful but rather dear these days. Walnut makes beautiful handles but is not as strong as the above. Oak does not look right in a handle and should be avoided because of its low tangential and radial strength. Finally there is a plethora of tropical and exotic species that work well. Rosewood is one of my favourites for small handles.

I often turn my handles from green wood. I chainsaw a good size green log to the proper length then rive billets from it. You want straight-grained green wood. If the log has been cut for any time discard the first 150mm 6″ to 305mm 12″, which will be checked, before cutting the actual piece to rive. Pick a section from the bowl of the tree that is straight and free of knots. A deep forest tree is best. Start by quartering the log with wedges. Depending on the diameter of the original log, you can work further with wedges or switch to a froe. The froe is an obscure tool used for riving and looks like a draw knife with one handle — bent the wrong way.

Fitting the Ferrule

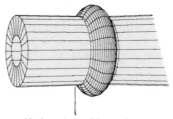

Undercut shoulder and cut slight groove

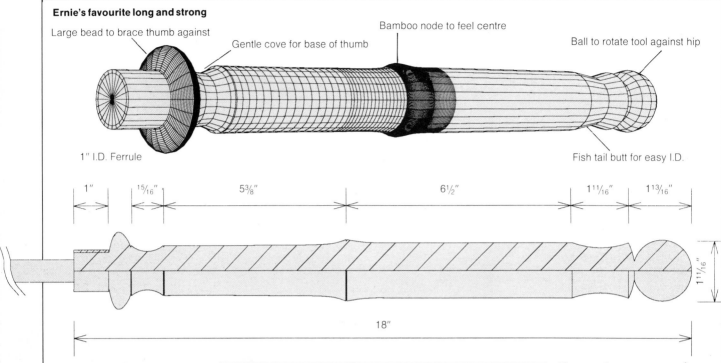

Ernie's favourite long and strong

Large bead to brace thumb against

Gentle cove for base of thumb

Bamboo node to feel centre

Ball to rotate tool against hip

1" I.D. Ferrule

Fish tail butt for easy I.D.

1" $^{15}/_{16}$" $5^3/_8$" $6^1/_2$" $1^{11}/_{16}$" $1^{13}/_{16}$"

$1^{11}/_{16}$"

18"

You place the froe precisely on the place you want to rive then tap it with a maul, which is no more than a giant carver's mallet. (A good turning project in itself!) Riving satisfactorily requires some knowledge of Newton's first three laws of motion. To rive straight you have to split equal masses. For this reason you need to keep dividing parts in half until you get the size billet you want. If you split unequal masses the split will walk in the direction of the lighter half. This has to do with mass versus acceleration and action reaction. It all sounds like a problem my old physics teacher would cook up.

Draw Knife

Once a billet is obtained of the proper size I work it to more exact size and roundness with a draw knife at the bench. Then it is merely a matter of chucking it between centres and turning a

handle. You cannot scrape green wood, it has to be sheer cut, but isn't that what spindle turning is about? You can sand a bit but I seldom do, as the finish of the tools is spectacular with green wood. You can also

If it looks good it probably feels good.

apply an oil finish at this time. As it seasons, the handle will become slightly egg-shaped but it will not check. This is because you do not have a complete annular ring in the billet, so it can stress relieve itself. Oddly enough the ferrule seldom comes loose either.

A handle from green riven wood is much stronger than its kiln or air dried, sawed cousin. All of the wood fibres are parallel in the billet and stretch from end to end. It also makes for a cheap

handle and the excess rivings, scrap and mistakes make good firewood. Helps to keep a handle on the heating bill.

Drilling

I drill my handles in the lathe. Simply mount a drill of the proper diameter in a drill chuck

in the headstock. Place the centre mark at the business end on the brad point of the drill and catch the centre mark at the butt end with the tailstock. Now start the lathe at moderate speed (300 to 600 rpm), hold the handle with your left hand and advance it slowly into the drill with the tailstock ram. You need to back out frequently to clear chips from the drill flutes. This is most important if the drill is

For odd handles inlet shank into two halves and glue together

not to bind and spin the tool in your hand. I put a piece of duck tape on the drill at the proper depth. With tapered tangs it is often good to step the hole. Simply drill for a distance with the largest diameter then work further with succeeding smaller diameters.

If you make your own tools you often have the problem of not having a proper tang. It is easy to find square and rectangular sections of tool steel that are hardened. With careful grinding, a splendid tool for some special purpose can be fabricated. To grind a tang, however, is time-consuming. This can be easily overcome by milling two billets that, glued together, will make a suitable handle. Now inlet the tool shank halfway into each piece and glue them together. I now insert a piece of hardwood scrap sawed to the size of the tool shank into the cavity for

turning. I catch this scrap with the extended centre, fit the ferrule and turn the handle to shape. Remove the scrap block and you have a custom handle that grew around the tool.

Well, that is about it. It is now time for you to get to the lathe and get a handle on your turning.   ∎

My dagger-type paperknife.

'Before you could say "Bleinau Ffestiniog", I had in my hand a nicely-turned handle attached to a one-inch, wafer thin, tattered blade'

Here's a simple project for beginners from David Womersley. Paperknives may not be the most exciting project, but they are one of the most useful. And you won't need a design degree to make them.

Strange, isn't it! Whenever you want to copy something you've seen dozens of times, the details flummox you. I was once making wooden fruit and couldn't remember how those wretched wrinkles around the stalks went.

So I sauntered off to the supermarket to find out. A sharp tap on the shoulder from the manager, no less, jerked me from my happy task. He asked what I was doing? "Oh, just looking at the wrinkles on your peaches and plums...well, to cut a long story short, I've got this fruit..."

But I digress. My project here is not fruit but paperknives, which have their own copying problems even though the design possibilities are fairly limited. Mine are the

FIG 1 Definition of terms.

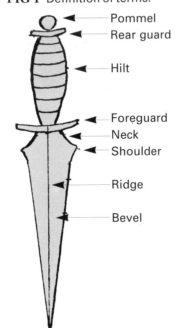

- Pommel
- Rear guard
- Hilt
- Foreguard
- Neck
- Shoulder
- Ridge
- Bevel

dagger type, pure and simple.

I make them in one piece, with the hilt about a quarter or one-third of the total length. The blade tapers not only from shoulder to tip, but along the section as well.

The guards, fore and aft, may be prominent or almost absent. The blade section may be rounded, or bevelled (ridged centrally). FIG 1 gives the names of the parts I've mentioned. I apologise if any are not technically correct, but at least you'll know what I mean.

Any close-grained hardwood, such as box, beech, yew, ebony, rosewoods, lime and sycamore, is suitable for this project. Avoid the fibrous, splintery types, as the blade edge will tend to break up.

FIG 2 The position of the initial cuts in relation to the design.

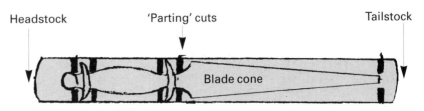

Headstock   'Parting' cuts   Tailstock

Blade cone

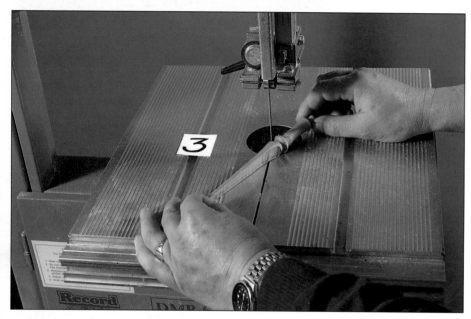

The hilt should be at the headstock end.

Cutting the blade. Hold the point in the right hand to act as a guide and steady. The blade guide is raised for clarity.

The author

David Womersley was born in Manchester in 1932 and has spent all his life in the North of England.
 He took early retirement in 1991 and a few years ago went on a two day course at Craft Supplies, and knew he had found the "something else" he had been looking for. Soon, his cellars had been converted from an odd-job area into a small factory, but there was nothing "factory-like" about his production.
The emphasis has always been on enjoyment rather than speed.
As with many fellow turners, craft fairs have been the chief way of selling his work. "Well, you can't keep giving it away, can you", he jokes.

The tools you will need are lathe, band or scroll saw, disc sander, drill and Velcro discs (37mm 1 ½" or 50mm 2"), fine triangular or half round files, and a carver's or Stanley knife. Oh yes, emery boards too, home made with strips of garnet paper (150 to 220 grit) glued to 3mm ⅛" thick strips of wood.

For those without a bandsaw, a fret-saw or coping saw will do, if you can muster a very delicate vice.

Method

For a typical 180mm 7" knife with a 22mm ⅞" foreguard, you first need to select a blank some 225mm 8 ¾" x 25mm 1". Bring it to the round between centres.

Pencil-in your measurements for pommel, fore and rear guards (leaving room for shaping), hilt and blade length. The hilt should be at the head-stock end.

Allow about 25mm 1" waste at the headstock and about half that at the tailstock end.

Shape the hilts and the guards with ³⁄₁₆" and ⅜" gouges, leaving the pommel to last. If the guards are to be concave, hollow-in with the toe of the skew. Usually, the hilt work can be completed, apart from the polishing.

Now for the blade. Shape this with the skew or gouge to a long, pointless cone (the blade cone), indenting the shoulder and neck below the guard as you go. Just taper the end down to about ³⁄₁₆" to ¼" at this stage.

Shape the pommel almost to a finish, steadying if necessary.

Pencil a line down the middle of the blade cone. Turn the cone through 180 DEG and draw another line down the middle. A card template may help here, if you're not happy doing it by eye. Remove the whole thing, waste and all, from the lathe. These pencil lines mark the position of the blade's 'cutting edge'.

Short break

Right, we'll take a 15 minute break here, to enable those without a band-saw or scrollsaw to rush out and grab the first person they see carrying one.

Meanwhile, the rest of us can down our vitamin pills with a cup of coffee, as the next bit is tricky.

OK, bandsaws at the ready, let's get back to work. Cut off the waste ends ▶

Photos: David Womersley and Healey Dell.

Check for trueness and turn the knife often.

Holding the knife with two hands, pass the blade over the revolving disc.

from the newly hatched embryo. You'll need to stand facing the side of the saw blade (10 to 14 tpi) with the guide fence removed.

Place the knife on the table, pencil-line up, so the saw touches the middle of the blade cone neck. The hilt, held in the right hand, is behind the saw blade and will be pulled to make the cut.

The point then, is in the right hand, which will act as guide and steady. Line the knife up at some 35 to 45 DEG to the table's centreline (depending on guard size).

Start the engine. Slowly pull the knife in an arcing cut towards the pencil line, to within 3mm - 5mm ⅛" - ³⁄₁₆" of it. Taper it gently towards the point, always keeping to the waste side of the line. Be careful to keep the whole thing upright.

Turn the knife over and repeat the process. The blade shoulder will be too thick at this stage. It can be trimmed with a couple of cuts from the front of the saw, but keep a good taper.

Don't be discouraged if you've ended up with an inside-out scimitar. Such knives are excellent for removing the middle from oranges etc.

We cut from the back for two reasons. One, cutting from the front, especially the thinner ones, could shatter the point, as it's almost impossible to support it safely.

Two, as the work is round in section,

there's a strong tendency for the saw to pull the whole thing over, unless it's supported at each end.

Now for 'grinding' and shaping the blade on the disc sander. I expect a belt sander will also do the job, but I don't know for sure, because I don't have one. Mine is a home made, lathe driven, 9" job. About 100 grit at 450 revs is the order of the day.

I remember, in a rash of enthusiasm, trying this stage of the work with 50 grit at 1100 RPM. Before you could say "Bleinau Ffestiniog", I had in my hand a nicely turned handle attached to a one-inch long, wafer thin, tattered 'blade'.

Hilarity

It was the source of much hilarity to my family. "New toothbrush, Dad?", or, "Great for opening short notes", was the level of wit I was subjected to. Ha, ha, very droll.

So keep it at 100 grit and 450 revs, if you want to avoid similar taunts from your own nearest and dearest.

Shape the point. Now angle the flat part of the blade to the spinning disc and, with short, vertical rolling movements, shape the section to the desired degree of roundness.

Bevelling is better done with a Velcro disc at the next stage. Check

for trueness and turn the knife frequently. Mind the guard.

The 'sharpening' comes next, using the drill and the Velcro discs. Mount the drill by its handle in the vice, with the Velcro pointing obliquely to the skies.

If you possess a fancy drill, select a fairly low speed. Holding the knife two-handed, pass the blade over the revolving disc, using a slow, rocking motion towards you, checking progress often.

If you want a bevel rather than a round section, substitute the rocking motion for one from side to side. Turn the blade often, and watch the guard.

It's almost inevitable that you will, at the very least, get some scuffing on the guard, or a few unwanted marks at the base of the neck. The files and 'emery boards' should remove these.

If too much wood is left at the base, the craft knife may be a better answer than to risk the whirling Velcro.

It only remains to go over the paperknife with 220 garnet paper, and to seal and polish in your usual way, before bearing your masterpiece to your wife for her gracious accolades.

"Very nice dear... What is it?", ∎

Show a leg

Photo 1 This collection of newel posts are all spindles, that is, between centre work.

Chris Pye describes how to turn table legs for a coffee or dining table, to illustrate the do's and don'ts of spindle or between centres turning.

Among woodturners, spindle turning is a shorthand way of saying between centres turning. This is because it's between the drive and tail centres that spindles are made.

Newels, table legs, bedposts, bobbins, and so on, are all turned in this way, the main difference being the different sized stock (Photo 1).

So, although I refer here to spindle turning I'm using the term in its broader sense to mean work between centres. A later article will look at the problems of a long, thin, spindly, workpiece – a stair baluster (p. 67).

Before that, I'll deal with turning an eight-foot bed post, to look at boring and joining wood. To start with though, I'm focusing on the between centres working of table legs.

I've taken these examples from actual jobs, and will describe my approach and methods of spindle turning, how I get pieces of work looking the same, how I keep concentration on a hundred of the same items, costing and so on.

I won't deal much with the actual cutting, as this has been well covered elsewhere.

The word spindle comes from the Anglo-Saxon spinnan, to spin (Concise English Dictionary). Originally meaning the actual pin or rod used for twisting the woollen thread in hand or wheel spinning, the word later came to mean any axis or arbor which revolves, or on which something revolves.
In the figurative sense it came to mean something, or someone, `spindly' – long or thin. So should you ever call a thin between-centres turner 'old spindle shanks' you would be applying an old Anglo Saxon pejorative in a particularly appropriate way.

I find woodturners tend to be split between those who prefer using only one (the drive) centre, for bowls or boxes etc, and those who go for work using both (drive and tail) centres, for legs, bobbins and so on.

This is not to say many turners don't happily combine one and two centre work. But this rough division illustrates that turning a chair leg between centres involves different tools and techniques to those needed to turn a bowl. And with this comes personal preferences and capabilities.

As a professional turner, I'm not allowed such luxuries as personal preferences. I have to satisfy my customers' needs, and many want some form of spindle turning rather than bowls or boxes.

One reason for this is that spindle turning usually forms a part, or parts, of a larger object – and is a common requirement of furniture makers, shop-fitters and joiners.

I'm not one of those wonderful time-served turners who have endless tricks and tales up their sleeves, but I do a good job, and have regular, repeat customers happy with what I make and prepared to pay for it.

There are other ways, I'm sure, of doing what I'll discuss in these articles, and little of what I am saying is new, but it works well for me, and I hope you'll find it useful.

The work

I'll begin with two sets of coffee table legs to be turned, then a small batch of handles.

The first, is a fairly simple cylindrical design in elm. I want to look at how I set up the lathe, make true cylinders and add the simple decorative beads.

My approach here, which seems to surprise some people, is that in turning such legs I use no marking aids or callipers, yet produce them in the quickest possible time and closely matched.

The set of legs in my next article (p. 28) moves onto a more complicated design which does need marking

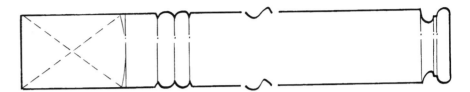

FIG 1 The table leg featured here has a simple but strong design, suitable for coffee or dining tables.

out and a certain amount of gauging.

Finally, I'll deal with a batch of tool handles, which involves boring and fitting ferrules as well as turning.

It's worth starting with a mention of 'down time'. This is the time when working directly on the job (in this case the coffee table leg) has stopped.

Down time happens whenever a turner changes tools, adjusts the toolrest, stops the lathe to alter the speed or replaces the finished turning with another blank piece of wood.

As I always get paid per finished item it's in my interest to complete the legs as fast as possible, so I try to reduce down time to a minimum.

It's not that down time isn't necessary. Sometimes it is unavoidable, such as the interval between a completed piece and a new blank. But down time is 'not-earning-time' in my eyes and I take pleasure (and profit) in finding ways of reducing it.

For these legs (FIG 1), and all my spindle turning, I start with wood as square-sectioned as possible and of exact lengths – either because I have dressed it myself or my customer has given it to me that way.

Why, I hear you ask, has a customer given me the wood, accurately square and to length? For two reasons: One, it usually pays him to supply the wood, as he almost certainly has bought a lot of it for the whole job – and I point this out to him.

Two, because I have trained him to square it up for me accurately. I don't moan or grumble, I tell him straight what I want when he first approaches me, and add that it keeps the cost down. It always works.

I mark the required pommels of the four legs together with a square (Photo 2) and put a centre mark in the

Photo 2 A simple rule is to do as many operations in a batch as possible to save time.

Photo 3 Once in position I don't adjust the toolrest at any time during the turning of the leg.

ends, marking all of one end at a time.

I use a plastic centre finder bought from Craft Supplies, finding this quick and accurate. If the wood is hard I will punch the centre points.

For a large number of legs I have various jigs for marking the centres straight away. I'll discuss these in a later article when I deal with runs of work. For just four legs I find the centre finder can be as quick.

I set the first blank between centres and position the toolrest. Photo 3 shows that I use a rest the whole length of the work.

I always arrange a single toolrest like this, covering all the points I need

▶

to turn, and at the most useful height. I hardly ever move it during turning. Only with larger work, say over 150mm 6" across, do I start finding the tool overhang a problem.

To stop and adjust the rest is down time. I have made a second toolrest holder (banjo) for my lathe, as well as metal toolrests of varying lengths which cover my range of work.

Most manufacturers supply only one toolrest holder and a limited length of rest which must be continuously adjusted.

The toolrest is positioned truly horizontal by eyeing through to the blank of wood, and then, by eyeing through to the bed from a position above, in line with the axis of the lathe (FIG 2).

The pommel is cut to shape (Photo 4) and waste quickly removed with a large roughing gouge. As this leg is cylindrical I plane a finished surface with a large skew chisel.

The trick here is to use the long toolrest, which I have carefully aligned, as a fence for my fingers to run along as they hold roughing gouge and skew chisel in a fixed position (Photo 5).

So no callipers are needed to get an accurate cylinder, and as the wood started nicely square it's easy to see and feel when an accurate cylinder is about to be reached with the roughing gouge and get a final sense of surface with the skew. The leg is a simple design so most of it is now finished.

Beads

Next come the details. The exact position of the beads was left to me. I always encourage customers to leave me some latitude in the design, allowing me to adopt quick approaches that look as if blood and tears have gone into them.

I estimated the width of the beads and coves by basing them all on the width of the same skew chisel with which I had smoothed the cylinder (FIG 3). The real advantage is minimizing down time.

Using the point of the skew, I made the first mark for the top bead exactly one skew-width from the pommel

(Photo 6) and the two next marks half a skew-width each (Photo 7).

So without changing tools, or resorting to dividers, I had the accurate marking for 2 beads, which I cut there and then (Photo 8).

It's important to be able to trust your judgement in this sort of case. I'm sure everyone can accurately estimate a half, or quarter, of their skew width. This is a real time saver.

At the other end of the leg I cut a bead in the same manner and marked a line for the width of the cove. Now I change tools, to a spindle gouge for hollowing the cove, and the toolwork is finished (Photo 9).

The leg can now be sanded. Here again, time can be saved by accurate tool work. You should be able to start the sanding at 180 grit at least.

This means that as well as using time-saving opportunities you must be able to turn well and efficiently. For this, of course, you need practice.

I take the leg from the lathe while it

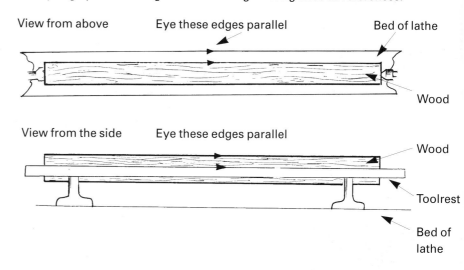

FIG 2 Eyeing up the full-length toolrest using existing lines as references.

View from above   Eye these edges parallel   Bed of lathe

Wood

View from the side   Eye these edges parallel

Wood

Toolrest

Bed of lathe

FIG 3 The skew 'unit'.

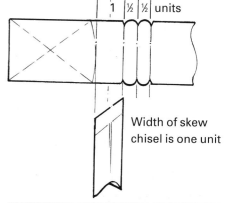

1 ½ ½ units

Width of skew chisel is one unit

Photo 4 Cutting the pommel to shape.

Photo 5 The neat cylinder is achieved using the toolrest as a fence along which to run the fingers, first with the roughing gouge and then with the skew chisel.

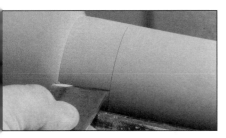

Photo 6 Marking one 'unit' with the skew into the smooth surface.

Photo 8 The beads are now finished.

Photo 9 I hollow the cove as well as create the small fillet with a spindle gouge.

Photo 10 To remove the leg from the lathe while it's revolving the wood must be drawn towards the tail centre and away from the toolrest. My thumb appears trapped but is in fact clear as I lift the leg.

Photo 11 Two finished legs. This simple way of estimating the positions of the beads and coves can be accurate enough.

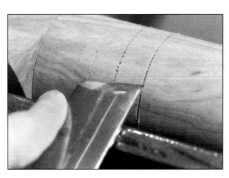

Photo 7 The second and third marks based on the skew width and I am ready to turn the beads without having changed tools or picked up dividers etc.

is still running (Photo 10). Many inexperienced turners find this a tricky and daunting prospect, especially where square pommels are involved. I do it to save time and because stopping and starting the motor tends to wear it out.

Holding the wood from below as it's removed I find the safest way, usually with my fingers around a bead or other grippable point. With my hand beneath, my fingers will always be knocked away from the toolrest and cannot be pinched.

As the tail centre is eased back, I both support the wood, and coax it away from the drive centre.

It's important the prongs of your drive centre are clean and sharp, or the workpiece will tend to stick to it. So if the wood won't come away cleanly, look to the drive centre for the answer.

Don't run the lathe too fast. I have mine about 1300 RPM for most spindle work.

When the turning has a square pommel, there's a danger of the corners hitting the toolrest and being damaged. In this case you need to ease the wood back both towards the tail centre, and away from the rest (Photo 10).

I centre the next blank of wood at the tailstock and ease the other end into the revolving drive centre, being careful to keep my fingers in the safe position beneath, as before. Then it's off onto the next leg. The whole process takes only a

The author

Chris Pye has been both a professional woodturner and carver over some 16 years. He started with carving, owing his formative introduction to the master woodcarver Gino Masero, and a little later added woodturning.
He considers himself self taught, and equally at home in both crafts, often combining them.
Chris was born in Co. Durham but has lived a large part of his life in the South West of England. He has several years' experience teaching adult education classes in woodcarving as well as private students in both turning and carving. In 1991 he demonstrated at the AWGB Seminar at Loughborough.
His first book, *Woodcarving Tools, Materials and Equipment* was published by GMC Publications last year.
Chris Pye,
The Poplars,
Ewyas Harold,
Hereford HR2 0HU.

This method of using the 'skew unit' can be accurate enough (Photo 11). As the four legs sit well apart in the table a little variation would be unlikely to be noticed, but it raises the question how close is close enough? This I'll look at in my next spindle turning article (p. 28). ∎

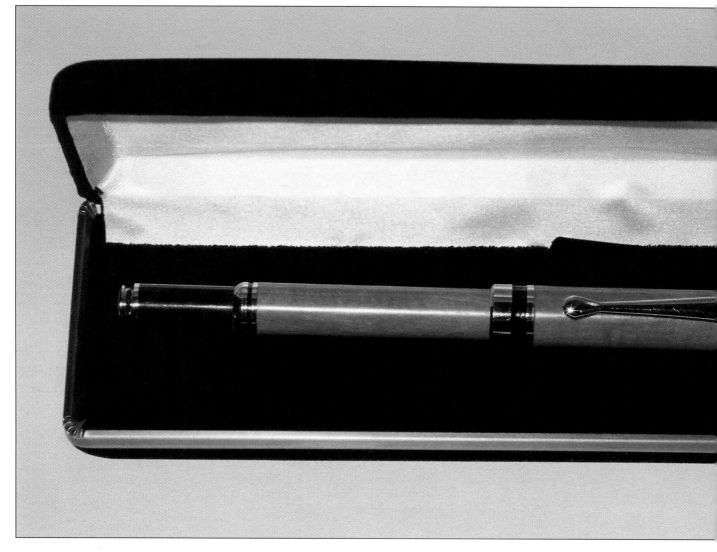

Woodturners wanting a break from the usual bowls, platters and candlesticks, might like to try their hand at these handsome wooden pens by Arthur 'Mac' Wilton

Wooden pens made from exotic woods are a bit like fingerprints – no two are the same. All have a different grain and figure, even though they are cut from the same piece of wood.

I've been making them for some years now and have found it an interesting and enjoyable project. Here's how I go about this delicate operation.

Stage One

Once you've decided on the type of pen you want to make, check all parts against the drawing supplied with the kit (Photo 1).

This helps to familiarise you with the various bits and pieces, the drill sizes and the procedures involved.

The type of pen I shall describe here is a propelling ball point from Craft Supplies, No.IB401 in their catalogue.

Stage Two

My favourite material for pen making is exotic woods (Photo 2), but other materials also give excellent results, including crushed velvet, bone, horn, imitation ivory and a number of plastics.

When selecting wood for the pen blank, particularly if this is your first attempt, it's advisable to select a close-grained wood, which will turn more easily.

Pen blanks come in the following sizes: small diameter 150mm 6" x 12mm ½" x 12mm ½", and large diameter 150mm 6" x 20mm ¾" x 20mm ¾".

Stage Three

The pen blanks are now numbered and marked out for drilling. If you prefer to keep continuity of grain, you should use some form of identification before dividing and sawing the blank into two pieces (Photo 3).

If you're only making one pen, you only need to mark a cross on each side of the dividing line, but if you plan to make more than one out of the same type of wood, then I suggest you use a numerical system (Photo 3).

Stage Four

Having cut the blank, you can now

▶

Pen craft

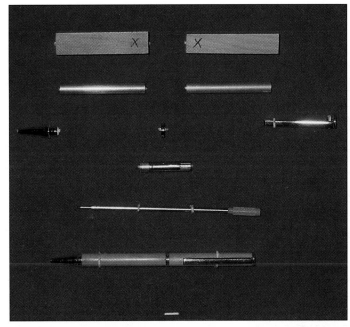

Photo 1 The parts needed to make the pen described here.

Far left:Photo 10 Pen made from pink ivory.

Photo 3 Pen blanks numbered and ready to drill.

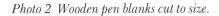

Photo 2 Wooden pen blanks cut to size.

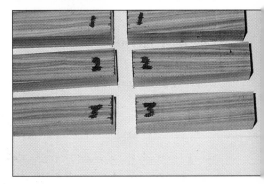

Photo 4 Ready to drill the pen blank.

The author

'Mac' Wilton is a retired electrical engineer whose main hobby is woodturning and woodwork in general.

He has learnt most of what he knows about the subject from books, magazines and videos, and also from the members of his local woodturning club.

His main interest is in spindle work, in particular working with exotic woods to create wooden-barrelled pens.

He lives in Lowestoft, Suffolk.

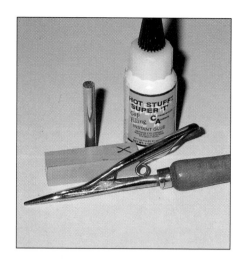

Photo 5 Pen blank, brass tube, adhesive and rug-making tool.

Photo 6 Inserting the brass tube with the help of the rug-making tool.

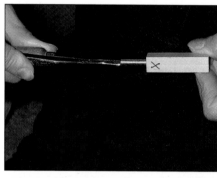

think about drilling the holes to take the brass tubes (Photo 4). This can be done in a number of ways, but the two I prefer are as follows:

1. Bench drill with the pen blank held securely in a modified machine vice.

2. Hold the pen blank in a four–jaw chuck in the lathe with the drill bit held in the tailstock. If you don't have a four–jaw, you may have to make up some type of jig to fit the lathe, or use whichever method suits you.

It's important to drill the hole as accurately as possible and not to drill at excessive speeds. You must also stop the drill at regular intervals to clear the drill flutes. High speeds and clogged flutes can generate heat which will cause cracking.

Stage Five

I've found the best adhesive for gluing-in the brass tubes is Hot Stuff, Super 'T', yellow label (Photo 5). This fills any gaps and allows 15 to 25 seconds for any adjusting that may be needed.

Take care to ensure it doesn't come into contact with your skin and eyes. I've found the ideal tool for holding

Photo 11 Pens made from tulipwood.

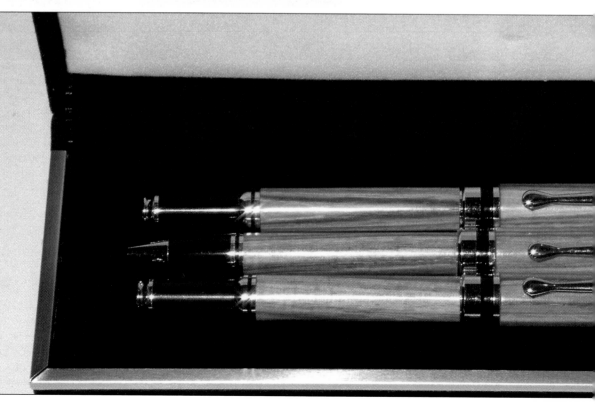

the brass tubes and then applying the glue is an old rug-making tool which I found at a car boot sale.

This has a spring lever which operates in much the same way as circlip pliers (Photo 6). I discovered this tool several years ago, and have found it very useful.

Before applying the glue to the brass tubes, clean them, if necessary, with wire wool. Then apply three beads of adhesive and, with a twisting action, insert the tubes into the pen blanks to just below the end of the blank.

Allow a short time for the glue to dry, then carefully cut and sand back the wooden blanks to the ends of the brass tubes. Now re-mark the wooden blanks, marking the inside of the brass tubes opposite the two crosses. We can then be sure of a grain match.

Stage Six

There are a number of specially made pen mandrels which simplify turning (Photo 7). It's advisable to buy one which will give good results (Photo 8). I select the highest speed on the lathe and use a ½" roughing

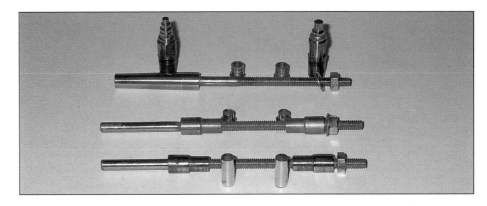

gouge, finishing with a ½" oval skew.

Aim at getting a good finish straight from the skew chisel, as this will avoid heavy sanding, which could result in cracking from overheating.

Try to get the outside diameter as near as you possibly can, as this greatly improves the pen's appearance. You now need to select a suitable finish, because the pen will be handled quite a lot.

I've found friction polish to be quite suitable, or sanding sealer finished with carnauba wax works well.

Stage Seven

We've now reached the stage I like best, assembly. First, ensure the ends of the pen blank are sanded square and lightly deburred (Photo 9).

All parts are made to a press fit, so you shouldn't need to use glue. A certain amount of force will be necessary to make the pieces fit. To press together, I use a bench vice with sheet material to act as jaw grips, such as Formica or melamine, to prevent any distortion when fitting.

I can't describe the assembly methods in general, because each type of pen varies in some small way. But for the type of pen referred to here, start by pressing the tip into one of the tubes as far as it will go.

Push the mechanism into the opposite end as far as the indent mark, and fit the ring over it. The refill can now be screwed in. It's sometimes necessary to file a small slot in the top tube to take the clip.

After this has been carefully done, push the clip and cap into the top tube and push the top tube into the mech-

Photo 7 A section of pen-mounting mandrels.

Photo 8 The blank mounted on a stepped mandrel.

Photo 9 Sanding the end of the blank square before turning.

anism to finish. You have now completed this interesting, and I hope enjoyable, project. Place it now in a presentation box (Photos 10 and 11).

You now have something which is not only beautiful, but functional as well. Your hand-writing will never be the same again.

All items used in this project are available from Craft Supplies, The Mill, Millers Dale, Buxton, Derbyshire SK17 8SN. Tel: 01298 871636. ■

Mirror, mirror, on a stand

Peter Symonds describes how to make a turning project with a difference – a circular, swivelling mirror.

If, like me, you like something a bit different, why not make a circular, swivelling mirror? Any glass merchant should be able to cut a round mirror to whatever size you want. The rest is straightforward woodturning.

The base is turned on a faceplate, to any kind of dish design and any degree of decoration you choose, but remember to leave a fairly substantial amount of stock at the perimeter, as it has to accept a decent sized screw

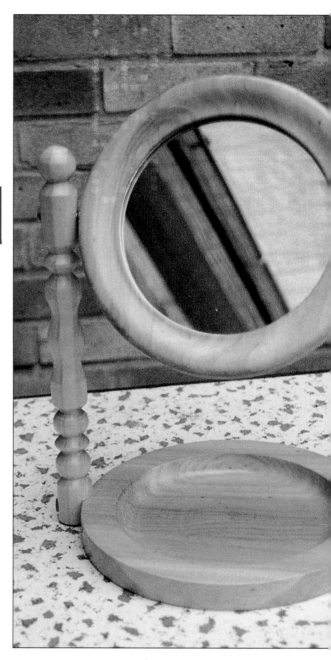

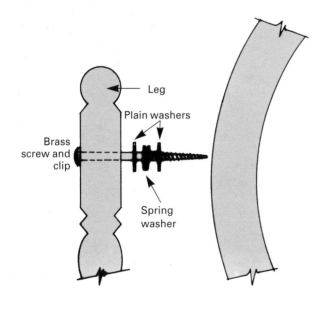

Leg

Plain washers

Brass screw and clip

Spring washer

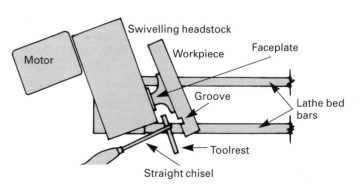

Motor

Swivelling headstock

Workpiece

Faceplate

Groove

Lathe bed bars

Toolrest

Straight chisel

Section of mirror frame

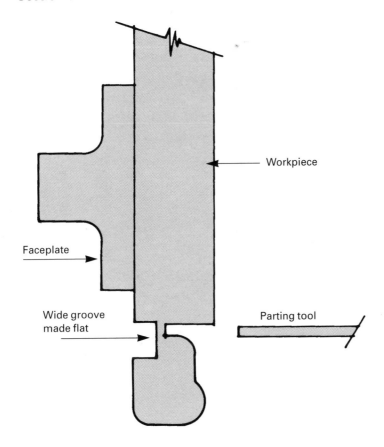

Workpiece

Faceplate

Wide groove
made flat

Parting tool

which will hold the legs on.

The legs themselves are turned between centres, again to any design which pleases you, but leave the bottom couple of inches, and a similar amount near the top, plain (see photo).

Notch the bottoms by up to half their thickness, and equal in depth to the thickness of the edge of the base. Plane two flats exactly opposite each other on the edge of the base to accept the legs, which are glued and screwed, using brass screws and cups.

The mirror frame is held in place with brass cups and screws passing through the legs. Before entering the screws into the frame, slide onto them a plain washer, followed by a split spring washer, then another plain one.

Screw up firmly, but not over tight, and you will find the spring washer will provide enough resistance to enable the mirror to be positioned at any angle.

The mirror frame is also turned on a faceplate. Try to get it out of one piece of wood. If you have to put two pieces together, take care to ensure a good glue line.

Remember, after the frame is turned, the glued area will really be quite small. Also, do make sure your timber is really dry.

I used Parana pine, which was not as dry as I thought, resulting in failure of the glued joint after about 12 months in a centrally heated room.

Trying to re-glue and cramp a relatively fragile circle of wood can be a bit tricky, if not exactly fraught with danger.

The mirror diameter is 200mm, 8", so the finished external size of the

frame needs to be about 250mm, 9 ¾". Having trued up the disc, you might like to put a bit of decoration on the edge, and perhaps round over the front and back corners.

Next, the rebate for the mirror and backing board. If you have a lathe with a swivelling headstock, such as the Thyme Avon which I use, by judicious swivelling of the head, and positioning of the toolrest, you can work the rebate from the back, that is, working on the same side as the faceplate.

In fact, what you will do is turn a groove, perhaps 20mm, ¾" wide, with an external diameter a little larger than the mirror.

Now go back to the front of the workpiece, shaping the face of the frame, and going straight in with the parting tool, to give an internal diameter about 15mm, ⅝" less than the mirror diameter.

The parting tool should pierce the work somewhere in the wide groove on the back, but if your intended finish is polishing on the lathe, don't go completely through yet. Leave a couple of millimetres, as sanding and polishing must be done now.

Take out a bit more stock towards the centre to facilitate this. Polishing complete, switch to low speed and finish parting, the tool held with one hand while the other is poised ready to catch the ring. A little hand finishing will probably be needed at this point.

The mirror glass is held in place by a thin ply or hardboard backing board, which in turn is held by fine panel pins. If desired, the back can be made as attractive as the front, by using a decorative disc, turned to a snug fit in the rebate, and glued in.

Alternatively, it could be fixed with a non-setting mastic, so that if the mirror is broken, it would be possible to remove and replace it.

If you haven't polished on the lathe, all that remains is to apply a few coats of varnish, and you have a very useful and attractive item, the like of which you will not find at any chainstore. ■

Johannes Volmer (Folmer) grew up in Dresden, the kings' residence of Saxony, famous for its baroque architecture, art galleries, china and museums.

Following the town's destruction at the end of the war, living conditions forced him, as a pupil and student, to work in several shops. The practical experience he gained of many kinds of handicraft and the machining of woods and metals led to his becoming a machine designer at Chemnitz, an industrial centre of machinery.

Johannes graduated from the Technical University of Dresden where he also gained higher degrees. His specialities are mechanics and design of mechanisms. He has taught these subjects for 30 years as a full professor at the Technical University of Chemnitz.

The country nearby, the woody Ore Mountains (Erzgebirge), is Germany's oldest woodworking region with ancient traditions and unique turning techniques still in use today. Woodturning is widely practised there. It was these circumstances that decided Johannes, some 17 years ago, to devote himself to the theory and practice of the almost forgotten art of oval turning. His studies resulted in his designing novel oval mechanisms which he tested himself.

Turning from the left is a special method of turning adopted in the early days by turners in the Ore Mountains (Erzgebirge) in Saxony, the traditional woodturning area of Germany.

Over the past few decades it was thought the use of automatic and semi-automatic machines would supplant it,

JOHANNES VOLMER

Turning from the left, a two-handed method particularly suited for low cost batch production, was used years ago by turners in Saxony, the German woodturning area. Prof. Volmer describes the method here.

LEFT TURN

Photo 1 Left-turning of slim columns of basswood (American lime in UK, American whitewood in USA) with a hollow ground skew chisel. Spindle turns clockwise.

but the method is still used for special turning jobs. It is a two-handed method particularly suitable for batch production at low costs.

Slender, long grained items such as lace bobbins or columns for Christmas pyramids — a traditional Ore Mountain decoration — but also buttons and pearls and the like, are chiefly produced on left-turning lathes.

Extremely small and thin components for musical instruments, figurines and parts for miniature figures can also be produced quickly and easily in small batches, without having

to make expensive tools for automatic lathes.

Left turning differs slightly from the usual method. The lathe headstock is situated — for right hand turners — on the right side of the lathe bed (Photo 1).

The headstock is fairly small and has slide bearings which, in turning very small parts, make the spindle run particularly smoothly. The spindle is running clockwise when looking onto the spindle head.

The toolrest extends along the entire length of the lathe. It is fixed parallel to the bed with its rim at the height of the

spindle axis (Photo 2).

The toolrest is made from hardwood, and its top rounded at the front. A steel strip to protect against wear and for better tool guidance is inlet inside the upper edge (Photo 3). The left-turner usually needs no tailstock.

When turning from the left, the turner sits at right angles to the lathe with his left side at the bed and his elbow resting on the bed behind the toolrest.

Tool guidance, the cutting process and the shapes of tool cutting edges hardly differ from those on the standard lathe. The tools are just shorter.

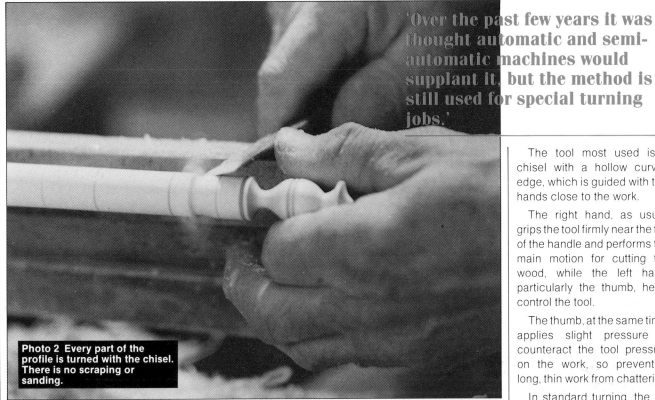

'Over the past few years it was thought automatic and semi-automatic machines would supplant it, but the method is still used for special turning jobs.'

Photo 2 Every part of the profile is turned with the chisel. There is no scraping or sanding.

The tool most used is a chisel with a hollow curved edge, which is guided with two hands close to the work.

The right hand, as usual, grips the tool firmly near the top of the handle and performs the main motion for cutting the wood, while the left hand, particularly the thumb, helps control the tool.

The thumb, at the same time, applies slight pressure to counteract the tool pressure on the work, so preventing long, thin work from chattering.

In standard turning, the left hand is freely held above the rotating spindle, but in left-turning the elbow rests on the lathe bed, so the left hand can reach up behind the work.

This elbow support, and the fact that the turner sits and guides the tool with both hands, makes him feel good and he acquires great skill.

He is then able to turn small pieces finer and faster by this special turning technique than by standard turning — sometimes even faster than an automatic lathe. Experienced left-turners can turn intricately shaped pieces very fast.

Left-turners use very sharp hollow ground skew chisels, cut the wood fibres and get smooth surfaces in unbelievably short times. There is no sanding necessary — the Ore Mountain turners of the past couldn't afford sandpaper.

The turning methods typical of this area are described clearly in the book *Drechseln in Holz* by R. Steinert, Leipzig: Fachbuchverlag 1990.   ∎

Photo 3 The left hand supports the long, slender workpiece to stop it vibrating. At the same time the fingers and thumb help control the tool held firmly in the right hand.

'The elbow support and the fact that the turner sits and guides the tool with both hands, makes him feel good and he acquires great skill.'

P R O J E C T

PETER SYMONDS

Born in Cambridgeshire, Peter Symonds now lives just over the border, in Suffolk. He is married with three children.

After training as a carpenter with a local firm, he served as a wireless operator, doing National Service with the RAF in Aden.

Peter has been in the building trade for 40 years, 32 of them as a self-employed builder. He joined the Ely Guild of Woodturners early in 1993 and says he has learnt a great deal from it.

Peter has been turning off and on since taking a short course in 1989, and uses a Tyme Avon lathe. He likes to try a wide range of projects, with the possible exception of miniatures, as his eyesight is not good. He's done a little carving, but adds that there are many things he hasn't had time to try yet.

Peter tries to recoup some of his expenditure by selling at occasional craft fairs.

'Derek didn't reveal his method until some time after the competition, when he gave us a demonstration. Meanwhile, I had developed my own, entirely different, way of doing things.'

Photo 14 The finished product.

Puzzle your friends with this variation of the captive cube on a thin-stemmed candlestick — the trapped triangle.

Trapped triangles

It was at an Ely Guild of Woodturners' monthly meeting where I first saw a captive cube on a thin-stemmed candlestick, shown to us by guild vice-chairman Derek Phillips.

Derek set a competition for members to make something similar, causing me to wonder what other shapes could be made on the captive ring principle. Pentagons and hexagons immediately came to mind.

As I had so far only made one half-decent captive cube, I decided a hexagon would take too long. And not knowing of any formula for setting out pentagons (perhaps readers could help me here), I settled on a captive triangle.

Derek didn't reveal his method until some time after the competition, when he gave us a demonstration. Meanwhile, I had developed my own, entirely different, way of doing things, as follows.

First decide on the maximum diameter and length of your candlestick, goblet or whatever you want to make. Allow 20mm ¾" or more waste at each end and turn it to a basic cylinder.

The cylinder must be exactly the same size at each end and straight, or even slightly concave, along its length.

Set a pair of compasses to the radius of the cylinder and use this to mark around close to one end, in the same way you would set out a hexagon (Photo 1).

Photo 1 Stepping out the hexagon.

Join up all these points across the end of the cylinder with a pencil, and transfer three alternate points along the length of the cylinder to the other end (Photo 2). Check this end with the

Photo 2 Transferring alternate marks to opposite end.

compasses, and again mark all points across the end.

One way to achieve a straight and parallel line along a cylinder is to do it on the lathe, using the toolrest close to the workpiece as a straight-edge (Photo 3).

Photo 3 Drilling points marked.

While the piece is on the lathe, mark a line around each end about 10mm ⅜" in (this measurement isn't critical), to cross each of the six hexagonal marks.

These are the positions for screw holes, necessary for attaching the cylinder to a jig, more of which in a moment. If possible, drill these holes on a bench drill, with the cylin-

der held in the drill vice.

A straight-edge can then be used to align the marks on the end of the cylinder with the drill bit (Photo 4).

I have used a pale wood (birch) and thick pencil lines for clarity, but for accuracy

Photo 4 And being drilled.

you should keep your setting out lines as fine as possible.

Throughout this exercise, accuracy is of great importance, otherwise your efforts will not result in an equilateral triangular prism, which is what you

should be aiming for.

Now for the jig. This consists of a disc of 18mm thick ply, the diameter of which must be greater than the length of the workpiece. Screw it to a faceplate and true up face and edge.

I use a heavy straight scraper for the face, which must be flat. Alternatively, you could turn a recess in the back of the disc and mount it on the expanding jaws of your chuck.

Cut a piece of scrap timber, square in section, about equal in size to the diameter of the workpiece, and of a length equal to the diameter of the ply disc.

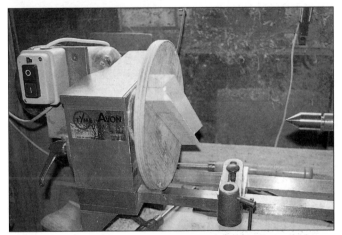

Photo 5 Disc and V block.

Make two 45 DEG cuts along its length, to form as large a V as possible. Mark across the centre of the disc, transferring the lines over the edge. Now centralise the V block on these marks and screw it on at one end only (Photo 5).

►

Photo 6 Sawing the triangular prism.

Photo 7 Not quite central....

Photo 8 ... *That's better!*

Photo 9 One face complete.

The other end is secured by screwing through a slotted hole from the back of the disc. This will enable the position of the workpiece to be adjusted sideways.

Centralise the workpiece lengthwise in the V and screw it on through the pre-drilled holes at each end. If you have worked accurately, the screws will enter exactly in the apex of the V.

The marks across the ends of the cylinder will assist

alignment. As the screws holding the cylinder will always enter the same holes in the V block, longitudinal adjustment should not be necessary.

Decide how much stock to leave at each end for the top and foot of the candlestick, and cut out the central portion, down to two of the pencil lines running along its length.

Repeat this twice, and the result should be a triangular prism with a short cylinder at each end. I do this by making multiple cuts on my radial arm saw, with the workpiece fixed to the V block, but before fixing both to the disc (Photo 6). It can, of course, be done by hand.

With V block and workpiece screwed to the disc, it's back on the lathe. Rotate the piece by hand while holding the point of a pencil against the cut face.

This will show whether things are central or not

(Photo 7). Make any sideways adjustments via the slotted hole (Photo 8).

Turn your design on one face, using whatever tools you deem suitable, sand and finish completely before rotating the piece to do the other two faces (Photo 9).

Make a note of the size of any holes, rings or shoulders which you turn on this first face, so that the other two faces can be made to match.

Photo 10 Tail centre cone in action.

It may not be possible to take measurements once the piece has been rotated.

It's easy to forget, when turning in this central area, that the outer part of the whirling circle is higher, but a rap on the knuckles will soon remind you.

Remove the piece from the jig, and the jig/faceplate from the lathe. Re-mount into a chuck in compression mode, using the tailstock centre to centre.

If you forgot to cut a spigot for your chuck jaws earlier, it

Photo 11 Ready for freeing off.

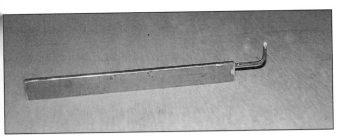

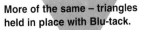

Photos 12 and 13 The tool to do it. Now for the tricky bit.

can be done now, as the centres will still be on each end. Replace the tail centre with a Jacobs chuck and drill bit and, using a slow speed, bore a hole for the candle.

Make it deep enough to allow for cutting off the waste with the screw holes in, which is done next. Turn and finish the top area, then bring up the tailstock to give added support.

CONE

If there is a likelihood of the tail centre point marking the work, I use a turned wooden cone, which is a snug fit over my revolving tail centre (Photo 10).

Now it's simply a matter of turning your candlestick to the desired shape, turning the stem thin enough to enable the captive triangle to be freed.

To keep the top and bottom ends of the triangle sharply square, I cut in very carefully with the point of a skew (Photo 11). I didn't have a suitable tool for the freeing-off operation, so I made one (Photos 12 and 13).

It consists merely of an Allen key, sharpened to a chisel point and hammered into a hole drilled in the end of a brass bar. It has since been improved by the addi-

tion of a wooden handle.

Any small ridges or roughness left inside the triangle can be removed with a small carving gouge. Tricky, but not impossible. Clean up the stem with a skew, sand and polish and there you have it, a captive triangular prism (Photo 14). ●

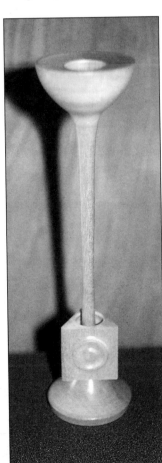

Here's one I made earlier.

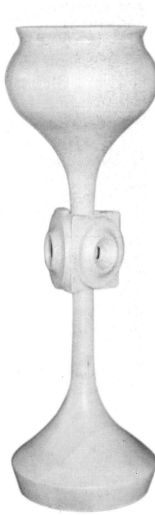

Maurice Mullins' love of wood, and interest in it, is lifelong. Two years studying at art school, ten years as an engineer/ technologist and eight years working in forestry and timber conversion culminated in 1982 with the decision to make woodturning a full-time business.

Being up to this time largely self-taught, he says "I decided to formalise my decision by completing a Start Your Own Business Course followed by one year on the Manpower Services Commission's Enterprise Scheme."

The award in 1985 of a Northern Arts equipment grant of £900 enabled him to update his lathe equipment and considerably boosted his confidence.

In 1987 he obtained a credit in the Open University Course *Design, Products and Processes*, and in the same year exhibited at the Harrogate (Trade) Crafts Show. This established the bread and butter side of his business.

In 1988 the award of a Northern Arts personal development grant enabled him to attend the opening of the International Turned Objects Show (in which a set of his goblets appeared) and also the third seminar of the American Association of Woodturners.

He exhibited at Loughborough in 1989 and demonstrated there in 1991. His many other notable appearances include a six-week residency at Grizedale Forest in 1990 where he worked alongside Merryll Saylan in demonstrating lathe skills.

Goblets in Miniature

MAURICE MULLINS

Maurice describes how to turn a $^1/_{12}$ scale love goblet with integral ring.

Miniature goblets made from cherry, holly, boxwood, cocobola and tagua nut.

W ell, I presume you have made many goblets since I showed you how in **Woodturning** Issue 6. I also hope you made a few mistakes! I still make mistakes as you will see later on — noboby is perfect. Anyway the challenge now is to make a well proportioned love goblet with a ring to $^1/_{12}$th scale, which is the scale commonly used when making a traditional doll's house. This means that if you have a normal life sized goblet say 150mm to 230mm 6" to 9" tall, then you will be aiming to make your goblet 12mm to 20mm $^1/_2$" to $^3/_4$" high. To get the scale divide 6" by 12 and you get $^1/_2$".

The tools and techniques can also be successfully employed on other small/miniature work such as dolls house furniture, scale models and lace bobbins. Before I go on let me dispose of a few myths that a lot of people including woodturners have about miniature turning.

1) It is not necessary to use a miniature lathe — the only advantage would be that a smaller lathe would run quietly and be more energy efficient than a medium to large sized lathe. The lathe I am using for this exercise takes 760mm 30" plus between centres and can swing 460mm 18" below centre. It is also the smallest lathe I

Selection of miniature tools made from whatever was handy.

have. What I do like about my lathe is that it gives me plenty of room to get my fingers underneath the tool rest to support the delicate work while it is being cut and to be able to catch it when parting off.

2) You do not need to buy special small turning tools — after all, will your hands begin to shrink just because you are going to turn small pieces? In the main I use standard gouges 10mm $^3/_8$" and 6mm $^1/_4$" DIA.

Some of you may prefer to use a shorter handle than normal but that's up to what works best for you.

3) The cutting techniques are not very different. The techniques I use on small turnings are largely the same as those I use on larger work. The cutting angle, the bevel and the degree of movement are the

same or similar. I am always looking for ways of cutting the wood with a slicing action. However this is not always possible and sometimes I use scrapers.

4) You do not have to use a magnifying glass. Fortunately I have very good eyesight. I have tried using a 100mm 4″ DIA. reading glass but without success. I do not like to work more than three hours turning miniatures as mistakes become repetitive probably due to a build up of tension.

Having disposed of those myths, we can now move on to preparing the materials and tools which you will need for miniature turning.

Materials: Close grained hardwoods such as box, maple, yew, holly, etc. should be easiest to deal with. You may want to try other materials such as cast resins, plastics, exotic woods, dried out seeds, tagua nuts and twigs.

Chucks: If you don't have a small collet chuck or drill chuck, a small faceplate with a block of wood will enable you to make jam chucks or a base on which you can glue the work-piece. Depending on your lathe design, it may be easy to jam your wood into the morse taper of the headstock.

Tools: It is not necessary to buy these (apart from a couple of gouges). They can easily be made from whatever is to hand — silver steel, masonry nails, push rods from old Mini engines, golf clubs, hacksaw blades, piano wire, even a 150mm 6″ nail. They say that necessity is the mother of invention. If you haven't got the tool, then make one — it's all part of the fun.

Lathe speeds: Whenever I am asked what speed should be used I always say whatever feels right. The fastest speed on my lathe is around 2800 RPM but on miniatures I prefer working at around 2000 RPM. I feel relaxed working at this speed. At 2800 the added noise of lathe and motor bearings doesn't help my concentration and can

Photo 1. Dividing the blank.

Photo 2. Instant goblet!

Photo 3. The blank from which the goblet was turned.

Photo 4. A 25mm 1″ blank of holly.

Photo 5. Slicing cut with the gouge.

Photo 6. A piece of tagua nut is glued on.

Photo 7. Even on this scale you should get shavings, not dust.

Photo 8. Small home-made hooked scrapers.

Photo 9. Round nose scraper made from a piece of wire.

cause a headache to develop.

Enough chat — time for work. Let's spend an hour or so in the workshop and see what can be done. My objective is to make a well proportioned scaled down version of a love goblet.

First of all we will make do without a chuck — I have rammed a piece of holly into the No 2 morse taper in the headstock spindle by carving the end of a blank 14mm 9/16″ square with a knife or chisel. The length of the blank protruding is approx 50mm 2″, so by using the tailstock support I can quickly produce a morse taper on the tailstock end. Divide the blank in the middle to produce your next blank (Photo 1). Then turn your goblet — just like that — easy I hear you cry! (Photo 2) I have left the goblet attached so you can see the amount of wood used to support the work (Photo 3).

For those of you that blinked,

this time I will try using a 25mm 1″ square piece of holly held in a collet chuck (Photo 4). The extra strength of the larger blank means you can turn with the workpiece well away from the headstock allowing you space to get your finger supporting the work from behind. As you can see I'm looking for a slicing cut with the gouge (Photo 5).

Oops! . . . Well I think I tried to cut too quickly and that's the end of that goblet. Ah well, never mind — this gives me the chance to try a glue chuck. The remaining holly blank is cleaned up leaving a flat end on which to glue a ready sawn up piece of tagua nut. Using gap-filling super glue, the end of the tagua nut and the wood are given a dollop each and brought together. A quick spray with accelerator will hold the piece in place. After a minute or so I run a fillet of glue around the

joint and once again a dab of accelerator is applied building up a weld that has great strength — enough to keep it in place while we turn it (Photo 6).

Even working at this small scale, correct use of the gouge will produce fine shavings — as opposed to scraping — leaving behind a polished finish as the bevel rubs on the work (Photo 7). It's perhaps as well because power sanding is definitely out.

The hooked scrapers (Photo 8) are smaller versions of the tools used in normal sized goblet making. They are made from used chainsaw files because the tongue is soft steel and it can easily be filed to shape using a small 3mm 1/8″ DIA chainsaw file. Again I have a left and right hand tool for this job to give the correct cutting angles with clearance.

Don't forget to try and experiment and make tools to your own design. Photo 9 shows ▶

Photo 10. Take extra care for the final stage.

Photo 12. The lid makes a friction fit in the box being turned.

Photographs by Maurice Mullins

Photo 14. Chuck gives plenty of space to get a hand behind.

Photo 15. A 10mm ³⁄₈″ square blank in the chuck and tailstock.

Photo 11. A lid turned from the remains of the tagua nut.

Photo 13. The outside of the box is turned to shape.

Photo 16. The blank is rounded and parted in the middle.

Photo 17. Inside is shaped with a 6mm ¼″ sharp gouge.

Photo 18. Outside is cut with the same gouge.

an attempt to cut the stem using a round nose scraper made from a piece of piano wire (usually available from model shops). I will have to make more cuts with this tool before deciding if it is an improvement on a small pointed gouge I normally use.

When you reach the final stage (Photo 10) remember to be careful — parting off is the most difficult part in making these goblets. I use a scaled down parting off tool that is sharpened with a slight skew. I don't part off completely with this tool. To finish I use a sharp pointed masonry nail which leaves a clean base. To try to clean up a nib on this size of workpiece is asking a lot.

While cutting away to make a fresh blank I made a lid with the remains of the tagua nut forming the finial (Photo 11). I was curious to test the strength of the glue joint — it was excellent. I then used the lid to make a box to fit which was big enough inside to house the tiny goblet I'd just made. The inside of the box was opened out roughly to shape with a small gouge then finished using the small piano wire scraper at an angle of 45 DEG. A 6mm ¼″ square-ended HSS scraper cut the slightly tapered rebate to

give a good friction fit lid (Photo 12). The outside of the box is shaped to suit (Photo 13), lightly sanded and polished using vegetable oil and 600 grit wet and dry. I do apologise, I have lost sight of my original objective. My only excuse is creative play — you just never know where a piece of wood will take you.

The chuck I use more than most is a standard 12mm ½″ drill chuck with a No 2 morse taper to fit the headstock of my lathe. This chuck gives me plenty of room for my hands to support the work if needed (Photo 14). A sharp tap with a copper mallet is enough to hold the chuck in position. Blanks are cut from 10mm ³⁄₈″ square wood, again shaping the end that goes into the chuck with a knife. The tailstock end of the blank is centred and marked with a sharp pointed awl (Photo 15).

There is enough wood to make two blanks so the square section timber is quickly rounded along its length and parted in the middle to give you another blank to use later on (Photo 16). The inside of the cup is shaped using a 6mm ¼″ gouge sharpened fairly acutely (Photo 17).

The outside of the cup is cut

Photo 19. Mini parting off tool cuts the disc for the ring.

Photo 20. Hook tools for cutting the ring.

Photo 21. Cut from the headstock side and the ring frees itself.

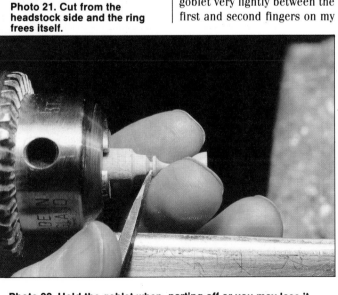

Photo 22. Hold the goblet when parting off or you may lose it.

Photo 23. The goblet with £1 coin for scale.

with the same gouge (Photo 18) or sometimes I use the larger 10mm ⅜" gouge as I find I get more control with the longer handle in` getting the shape smoothly cut without any flats or ridges.

The miniature parting off tool I made (Photo 19) cuts the disc that will hopefully make the ring. Photo 20 shows the two tools I've developed to cut the inside of the ring from the left and the right. The outer edge of the ring can be shaped only by sanding lightly with 400 grit wet and dry.

Carefully cut into the disc from the tailstock side. You do not want to go right through at this point or the ring will look very clumsy and may well break up. Cutting from the headstock side the ring will eventually free itself (Photo 21). While cutting the stem I find the use of a finger at the back of the workpiece may be useful in keeping the ring to one side while you cut the other side. Two fingers (Photo 22) are very useful when it comes to parting off.

The base has been cut using the mini skew parting off tool and fed in to provide a concave base so that the goblet will stand on its rim. Continuing with the cut right through to the middle will probably send your prize goblet into orbit unless you can catch it. I hold the goblet very lightly between the first and second fingers on my left hand as shown.

Believe you me, you can spend hours looking for a dropped goblet in the shavings. So a quick photograph of the finished article before I lose it (Photo 23). I've just had a thought — for those of you who can't use my method, try tying a piece of cotton to the ring and don't forget to tie the other end to your tool rest. I haven't tried it yet but it sounds feasible.

Well there you have it, the end of a session and some more goblets for your collection. We

Collection of love goblets.

have covered making the goblet, making the tools to make the goblet, three different methods of holding the work, and at least one idea to try out in future. Don't despair if you break a few — eventually it will come. I've just seen some photographs of my first attempts at goblets and they make me cringe with embarrassment.

If you get the chance, have a look at *Lathe - Turned Objects* (The International Turned Objects Show catalogue) and look at the work of Clead Christiansen, J. Paul Fennel, Wilmer L. Senlt and Stephen Paulsen's *Wall Constructions* — magic! ∎

Spindle shanks

In the second part of his spindle turning mini-series, Chris Pye describes how to turn coffee table legs and tool handles.

I n my last article (p. 8) I turned a set of four fairly simple table legs, telling how, for business reasons, I minimized 'down time' by completing them as fast as possible.

I did this in the following ways, by:
- Starting with well prepared, good quality timber, and getting the customer to prepare it.
- Not switching the lathe off and on.
- Having a toolrest that extended the whole length of the work piece.
- Not adjusting the toolrest at any time while turning.
- Changing the tools the least number of times
- Finding quick ways of marking the design on the piece and avoiding callipering.
- Crisp toolwork that minimized sanding time.

It may be, however, that you, your style and approach to turning, will find other, better ways of saving time – in which case let us know.

On the other hand, particularly if you're in the early stages of your turning career, you may find some of the above impossible to achieve.

For example, you might have to put up with inferior material from a customer, or you cannot afford the extra length of toolrest. Perhaps removing wood while the lathe is turning or working with a deep overhang feels particularly hazardous, or perhaps your toolwork needs more practise.

All you need to do is *keep trying* to improve and, one by one, bring in these techniques. Get in plenty of

> **'You should always take advantage of your knowledge when dealing with customers. I've never known it not to be appreciated, and it benefits you as well'.**

Photo 1 Coffee table legs in Douglas fir.

practise time and learn to trust your hand and eye.

The next item of spindle turning I'm going to look at is another set of coffee table legs, but of a more elaborate design.

Question

I'll look a little more at how to get these four legs the same – which begs the question what is this 'same' you are trying to achieve? How close do two turned items need to be?

Let's start by turning the legs. I've made mine in Douglas fir (Photo 1).

The wood was well prepared to size and length, the end centres and pommels quickly marked, the first piece

offered to the lathe, and the toolrest adjusted to allow me to work on all the turned section at the same time.

If everything has been arranged well, the wood will spin with a neat blur of the edge. I cut the pommel with the skew, roughing out the cylinder as before. As the toolrest was aligned with the bed of the lathe I turned the gouge on its side and, using the rest as a fence to run my fingers along, arrived at a clean cylinder.

The junction with the pommel I cleaned with the skew, planing only a small, adjoining part of the cylinder.

A section of cylinder is often left next to a square pommel in most items of spindle turning, as it keeps

Photo 2 Take the profile for subsequent legs from the first. It's a quick marking method, taking no more than seconds per leg, once the gauge is made.

Photo 3 Score grooves at important junctions with a triangular file. Don't bother with fillets, they can be created as you turn.

Photo 4 Marking the wood with a point resting in the grooves.

Photo 5 I calliper a width to the side of the bead I will cut later.

the subsequent tool (usually the skew) away from the corners of the pommel.

A bead here will need a parting chisel to shape the side away from the pommel – an extra tool.

The design was given me by the customer, but I usually suggest little changes to help with the turning or the design, such as the leaving of a small section of cylinder next to the pommel.

Knowledge

You should always take advantage of your knowledge when dealing with customers. I've never known it not to be appreciated, and usually it benefits you as well.

With the customer's sketch to hand, I worked out and finished the first leg. As these legs were more detailed than the last set, I needed the well-known marking gauge to match the other three (Photo 2).

These gauges take only a few minutes to make and are worth keeping as

a reference for future work and discussions with customers.

I always mark important diameters on the gauge and note anything important about the work on the back. In this case the important diameter is the lower bead, which is narrower than the one at the top.

The gauge takes as its reference point the pommel on the left and lines up all the features accurately in a profile (Photos 2, 3 and 4).

Make sure that when the gauge is put to the new wood it's placed uniformly against the spinning pommel.

The turning is fairly straightforward, but there are a few points of note in the context of working as quickly as possible.

Immediately after marking the relevant lines with the gauge, I use callipers to get a level for the lower bead (Photo 5).

Waste

You can see I chase the level on the waste side of the final bead. I then eye this level as I work the bead down and the waste away with the skew (Photo 6).

This is the only time I need callipers. To get the lowest diameter of the foot I use my eye again, relating the wood to the known size of the tail centre. In this case the two diameters are the same, so it's a relatively ▶

Photo 6 The bead formed and the sides trimmed down to fillet level. If I always cut the bead in the same way then the fillets will always lie at the same level.

Photo 7 I go as far as I can with the skew chisel, shaping into the hollow below the fillet.

Photo 8 I take the lowest diameter of the foot from the diameter of the revolving tail centre.

Photo 9 A quick cleaning up into the hollow is sometimes needed. This is an extra tool, so I avoid it if I can, but I'd rather cut than sand.

Photo 10 The two legs are very alike.

straightforward eyeing across.

I go as far as I can with the skew chisel (Photo 7). The top bead and belly of the leg I do by eye, with the original leg in front of me.

The coves finish off and here I need to change to a spindle gouge (Photo 8). I may need to touch up the belly to cove join with the skew again (Photo 9).

The leg is finished bar the sanding, which can start at 180 grit.

The method of replacing the finished leg with a blank is described on page 10, so it's off with the finished leg and on with the next.

As with the previous set of legs, I minimized the use of different tools and callipering where possible, relying on eye and tool work to get details the same.

As a guide, each leg, except the first, took about four minutes and I could sense the time reducing as I got into the swing. But, after four the job was finished, just when I was warming up.

Speeding up on later items is important if a turner is to get back slower time spent at the beginning.

Spindle turning usually involves more than one item. For example, most tables and chairs have four legs, and stairs have several newel posts. It's quite usual for beginners to produce a very creditable single item, but to have difficulty in matching it throughout the set.

I've seen this inability cause potential spindle turners to become bowl turners. So, how *do* you get four the same?

Tools

First you must know how to use your tools. By this I mean *you must be able to get the shape you want.* I've lost count of the number of table legs or spindles I have turned – which means I have done a lot of practise.

Practise is what's needed, even to the point of setting yourself exercises. I ask students who profess to be serious about turning between centres to turn a given number of beads and coves a day, in different sizes and combinations.

One hundred beads or coves a week is 5,000 a year. This is like pianists working to perfect their scales; training the 'body memory'. There's no substitute for intelligent practise.

The second point is to turn each leg, *using the same tools, in the same way, each time*. So, in our example, I cut the top cylinder in as true a semi-circle as I can down to a depth which either relates to the width of the skew, or is just one I feel for.

Rounding the belly of the leg in from another set point automatically gives the same shape (Photo 10).

It's not unusual for the last leg of a large batch to be a little different to the first – this is simply due to a settling down into a style and approach of using the tools.

Quick dressing

Be prepared to pop the first couple of legs back on the lathe for a quick dressing. I suggest you keep them separate, but if you can't find them in the mass of other legs you probably don't have a problem.

An item which is 'hand made' implies a degree of human variation. But how much is permissible? (Photo 11). I had one customer making reproduction Elizabethan furniture who complained that I was never rough and inexact enough, as if the Elizabethans were.

In all the years I've been working, no one has complained about a little variation. On the contrary, owners are pleased to have handmade work. That's why they are at my door and not the man with the automatic lathe.

They will usually be prepared to pay that bit more when it is obvious what the benefits in quality are with hand work.

If items, such as candlesticks, are to be seen close together, with time to be contemplated, they need to be closely matched. The tolerance in legs seen far apart can be a bit more. But you should always try and match as closely as possible. So beware the mechanical, train the hand and eye.

Sometimes the items need not be matched closely, but still need to be

▶

Photo 11 Another set of legs. You must be thoroughly competent with your tool work before you can happily churn out runs of items all the same.

Photo 12 Tools with ferrules and wood for handles, all sorted and ready.

Photo 13 Boring a handle. I used the same pilot bit even though some of the tangs were larger.

Photo 14 All bored, ready to shape.

Photo 15 Using the side of the roughing gouge to come close to the ferrule diameter.

Photo 16 Sizing for the diameter. I do all the same sized ferrule handles together.

Photo 17 The ferrule is a snug fit. Note the lathe is still running.

Photo 18 All the rest of the turning is with the skew, parting off to length, again without stopping the lathe.

Photo 19 The finished handles.

The author

Chris Pye has been both a professional woodturner and carver over some 16 years. He started with carving, owing his formative introduction to the master woodcarver Gino Masero, and a little later added woodturning.
He considers himself self taught, and equally at home in both crafts, often combining them.
Chris was born in Co. Durham but has lived a large part of his life in the South West of England. He has several years' experience teaching adult education classes in woodcarving as well as private students in both turning and carving. In 1991 he demonstrated at the AWGB Seminar at Loughborough.
His first book, *Woodcarving Tools, Materials and Equipment* was published by GMC Publications last year.
**Chris Pye,
The Poplars,
Ewyas Harold,
Hereford HR2 0HU.**

produced quickly. The next job was one such – nine handles for some carving tools.

Issue 13 of *Woodturning* has full details of turning any single handle. Here I will look at how I deal with a small run.

Tool handles

I always keep blanks of interesting woods, bandsawn to roughly the same size, in a box. I select a ferrule and piece of wood for each tool and line them up ready to go (Photo 12).

I don't mark the ends. The wood is a little rough but oversized so there is some leeway here. I bore the batch all together with a small pilot bit (Photo 13 and 14).

For shaping, the blanks are reversed so the pointed tailstock goes in the hole. As before, once positioned, the toolrest is not moved.

When the handles are roughed to an estimated diameter I use the side of the roughing gouge to get a diameter for the ferrule (Photo 15). This is then 'sized' and the ferrule fitted (Photo 16 and 17).

I do all the same sized ferrules at the same time and estimate the length

needed for the ferrule using the known width of the parting tool in the sizing gauge. This is similar to the approach I took with the skew in the previous issue.

Then the handle is finished with the skew and parted off to a length. I get the length and shape by feeling the handle with my hand (Photo 18).

Note the lathe is never turned off. In a professional workshop a lathe can go for hours without being switched off, so it obviously needs a strong motor.

The next handle is offered up and the process repeated until the batch is finished (Photo 19).

In this example, the same principles of minimizing down time are applied, including:

■   Trying to use the same tool or set up for as long as possible.
■   Not changing anything I can get away with not changing.
■   Not measuring anything I can gauge by eye.

In a job like these handles a degree of relaxation from the shaping discipline makes it feel like a bit of a holiday.

There's no doubt spindle turning

takes a lot of discipline, and that probably means some people are more suited to it than others. But it has a wide range of applications.

In the next article (page 45) I will look at assembling a long spindle – a fourposter bedpost – and taking in the boring of holes and marrying of spigots.

■

THE SHAPE OF MY THINGS TO COME

RON KENT

'As I look at these bowls the silhouette seems to converge to a vanishing point just above the supporting surface. To me, the bowl seems to float.'

Ron Kent is a man of many parts. He is a veteran stockbroker, an adult education teacher, a call-in radio talk-show host on personal finance and investment and a conductor of seminars on personal finance and creativity. Not least, he is a woodturner whose beautiful translucent bowls are in private collections worldwide. Oh, and we almost forgot, he lives in Honolulu, Hawaii!

Today I'm going to do something much more difficult than designing an attractive bowl. I'm going to discuss the design *process*. More precisely, I'm going to describe the evolution of the 'new' profile that now influences most of my current woodturning.

First a little 'preview', and some background. By now you've glanced at the pictures. The shape isn't really that radical, is it? I realize that most of us have made goblets and chalices at one time or another, so there is nothing new about either the format or the technique. This shape has three basic components: a bowl, a neck, and a base. Most often when we make them our scale and shape are approximate to those of the wine glass or brandy snifter.

'Scale'? Hey, scale is a fourth component, one that is taken for granted. Wine glass, goblet, snifter, chalice . . . all fall within a narrow range of sizes: small. Oh, I've ventured larger from time to time, but when doing so, I scaled up all of the components proportionately. I simply made a **big** brandy snifter. When the lip of the bowl got up to 510mm 20″ in diameter, the neck would be as much as two inches.

AESTHETICS

Let's leave the goblet discussion for a moment and trace the evolution of my personal sense of aesthetics.

It's easy to recognize what influenced my early bowl designs: the kitchen cabinet! All the bowls I had been seeing through all of my life before then were bowls that had been created to be USED! Pyrex, pottery, plastic, or wood, they were solid, stable and utilitarian. These no-nonsense bowls were as unshakeable as the surfaces they stood on.

But beauty will out. Though pedestrian in shape, the beauty of the medium just would not be denied. Even as I worked with the whorls and knots, I started seeing how slight change in shape might emphasize the characteristics of the grain. Instead of knowing

before I started, I now designed each bowl as I learned more about that particular piece of wood. Originally I saw my challenge as making the largest possible bowl out of each log. Today, even if it means wasting much of the log, my goal is to make the most beautiful.

Beauty, trite but true, is in the eye of the beholder. I soon learned that my own idea of beauty tends strongly to thin walls and slender bottoms. The diminished diameter base became a 'signature' characteristic of all my bowl designs.

The bottoms of my bowls were certainly narrow by traditional criteria, but they still left me with a nagging sense of dissatisfaction. I didn't like interrupting the gracefully flowing lines of the bowl to accommodate even that tiny base.

AMPHORAS

Perhaps I was influenced by the ancient Greek amphoras. They

255mm 10″ H x 460mm 18″ Diam

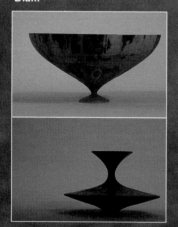

255mm 10″ H x 255mm 10″ Diam

'Originally I saw my challenge as making the largest possible bowl out of each log. Today, even if it means wasting much of the log, my goal is to make the most beautiful.'

typically have no 'bottom' as such, but converge to a rounded or slightly blunted point. To remain erect, the amphora requires a supporting stand. I tried that combination and felt it did not translate well to wood.

I also tried variations of 'legs' but found that equally unsatisfying.

Recently I got another idea and put it to the test. I would indeed taper down toward the amphora's blunted point, but not quite complete it. Now I had to determine how slender and short a neck would be needed to support the bowl firmly but inconspicuously. What shape and size base would I need below the neck to fulfil these same requirements?

It took very few trials to convince me that the idea works and to find proportions that pleased me. My typical neck has a diameter of 12mm ½". The base need be no broader than 100mm 4" in diameter, (even on a 610mm 24" bowl) and no thicker than 20mm ¾" where it joins the neck.

I won't defend the practicality of this design since my consideration was aesthetic rather than utilitarian. The question was whether or not I would like it. When I made the first such bowl I wasn't at all sure that I did. Fascinated by it, to be sure. Kept looking at it; couldn't stay away! But did I **like** it? By the end of three weeks there no longer was any question in my mind. This, I knew, is the shape of things to come.

PEDESTAL FORMAT

For the past few months I've continued to adapt this 'pedestal' format to my full range of size and shape. Deep and shallow, vertical and horizontal, little and large . . . all seem to me to show to good advantage in this format. As I look at these bowls the silhouette seems to converge to a vanishing point just above the supporting surface. (I don't even notice the neck.) To me, the bowl seems to float.

The birth of a 'pedestal' bowl

Older and new profiles. Same wood — Hawaiian Mild

200mm 8″ H x 560mm 22″ Diam

230mm 9″ H x 510mm 20″ Diam

TECHNIQUE

I'm not quite certain how other woodturners would make one of these bowls, but I'll tell you how I do it. My normal technique, you may realize, is to do all of my work between centres, rather than with faceplate. (I use hand-tools to remove the remaining stems after my completed bowl is taken off the lathe.) So . . . I do everything in my usual fashion, completing the bowl inside and out, except for the 'neck' itself. This I leave for the final lathe operation. I find that a 25mm 1″ diameter neck allows me to visualize the final configuration yet is strong enough to proceed normally with shaping and . . . you should pardon the expression . . . sand-papering.

If, like me, you are going to use a tailstock, be careful to avoid excessive pressure. I like to force the tailstock into the log, then back off a quarter-turn for this purpose.

In writing this article to tell you about my new direction, I've learned a little more about myself. Yes, I like this new format and find it very pleasing. And yes, I design and create my bowls to my own standards and satisfaction. But will I keep using this design if it turns out that I'm the only one who likes it?

What do you think? ■

GÖRAN SÄTTERSTRÖM

Hundreds of boxwood and ebony bottle boxes were made in this country during the last century, but here Swede Göran Sätterström describes his own unusual method for encasing a glass bottle with wood.

Göran Sätterström, 51, lives in the south of Sweden, near the Baltic town of Karlskrona, which hit the headlines in 1981 when a Russian submarine was stranded just outside it.

He works as a full-time consultant in soil mechanics and foundation engineering.

Göran's interest in wood goes back to his early childhood, when his father and a neighbour taught him to turn on an old cast-iron lathe.

He doesn't see himself as a master turner, rather someone who gets "a lot of more or less crazy ideas" which he tries to realise on the lathe.

Most of the ideas, he says, are too crazy and end up in total disaster. "But if you don't fail you don't learn."

In his turning, he tries to adjust the form to the type of wood being used. A big bowl in delcate cherry should be rather thin with a smooth form, he says, while a bowl in Swedish pine can be rough in form.

Göran adds that the turning point in his turning came when he discovered English books on the subject. In Sweden, he says, there is just one book worthy of the name of woodturning literature.

He is convinced a lot of Swedish woodturners would welcome the translation of English books.

WOTTA LOTTA BOTTLE

A 'woodturner's bottle'.

For aeons, glass bottles have been covered in materials of various kinds. Some have been encased in leather, others with tarred strings of hemp (seamen's bottles), birch bark, or whatever. The aim has always been twofold — to protect and enhance the bottle.

A woodturner should, of course, have his bottle covered in wood. But how do you make it? Here is one answer, although I am sure there are others.

First you need a suitable bottle. It should be round with a longish neck and a fairly straight body having, preferably, only one curved part (FIG 1).

It can have a more curved body, but this makes things much more difficult. The cap should be a screw type of metal or plastic. An ordinary cork will do, but in the end it will wear out.

Then you need a piece of wood. This must be of a kind which is very stable and unlikely to distort because of temperature and moisture ▶

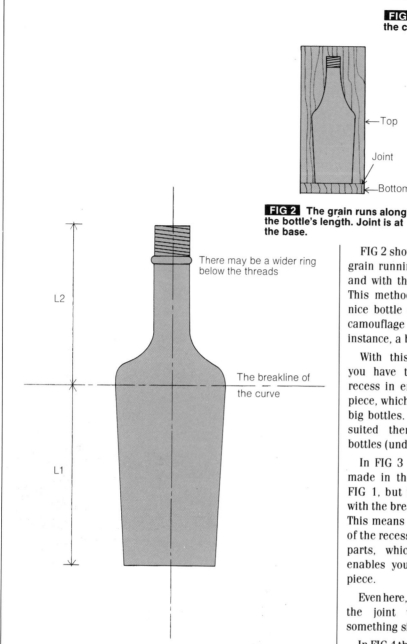

FIG 3 The joint is in line with the curve's breakline.

FIG 2 The grain runs along the bottle's length. Joint is at the base.

FIG 4 Laminated sections disguise the joint.

There may be a wider ring below the threads

The breakline of the curve

FIG 1 First you need a suitable bottle.

FIG 2 shows a bottle with the grain running along its length and with the joint at its base. This method produces a very nice bottle cover and you can camouflage the joint with, for instance, a bead.

With this method, though, you have to turn the whole recess in endgrain in the top piece, which is a bit difficult in big bottles. It's a method best suited therefore to smaller bottles (under 150mm 6").

In FIG 3 the bottle cover is made in the same way as in FIG 1, but the joint is in line with the breakline of the curve. This means you can make half of the recess in each of the two parts, which is easier and enables you to turn a larger piece.

Even here, you can camouflage the joint with a bead or something similar.

In FIG 4 the bottle case is also made from two pieces, but each is assembled from small flitches of, for example, spalted birch. The grain runs horizontally here, and the flitches should, if possible, be quarter sawn.

In this method the recess turning is much easier, as you don't have to do it in endgrain. The finished case is, furthermore, so full of joints that you can't tell which is the main one. A laminated construction like this also makes it stronger.

You can, of course, use only two pieces of wood, but then a rather large log of dry wood has to be obtained for a big bottle. To prepare the two pieces, you can glue the flitches together (Photo 1).

Note the paper between the

Photo 1 Glue the flitches together.

bottom piece and the top piece, a safeguard against glue coming between the two main pieces by mistake.

Having chosen your bottle and wood, you need to make a couple of good templates, one for the inner recess and one for the outside curve. These can be made using a good adjustable profile gauge or in the following way.

First make a drawing tool from 5mm ³/₁₆" plywood. Then fix the bottle to a piece of cardboard on a flat surface, using a hot glue gun. Draw the bottle's outline. Note the line will be drawn about 2mm ³/₃₂" outside the exact line (FIG 5).

Now you make a drawing like FIG 6 (the inner line). This is the template for the inner recess, but don't cut it out for the moment.

To get the template for the outer curve, draw a second line outside your first at one side of the bottle. If you want the

content differences in the surrounding air.

The wooden case is bound to distort slightly for the above reasons, but the bottle inside won't. Remember this, otherwise the wood will almost certainly crack, sooner or later. It may be possible to use PEG, but I have not tried it.

I often use spalted wood such as spalted birch, for two reasons. First, spalted wood seems to move little compared to unspalted, though I'm not sure why. Perhaps the spalting pro-

cess affects the elasticity of fibres.

Second, spalted wood adds an extra touch to the appearance, especially if the bottle is a bit dull.

In theory, making a woodturner's bottle is easy. All you have to do is make recesses in two pieces of wood in the exact shape of the bottle, place the glass in it, glue the two pieces together, and turn the outside to the shape of the bottle inside. Simple, isn't it! But there are a few difficulties along the way.

FIG 5 Glue the bottle to a piece of cardboard.

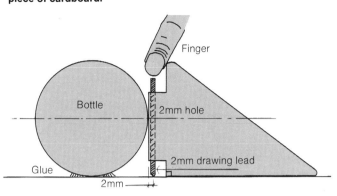

FIG 6 Templates for the inner recess and outer curves.

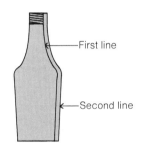

faceplate or another kind of chuck, but the later work will be much harder. If you do use a faceplate, the workpiece must remain screwed to it so that centricity is ensured when it is returned to the headstock spindle.

True up the end of the wood, but don't turn it round yet. Keep it square. Turn the recess with the help of your template. Be sure to get it exact, not too wide and not too small.

The breakline of the bottle should be perfectly in line with the trued up end (Photo 4).

If you have been thorough you should have a good fit, with about 2mm $\frac{3}{32}$" of space between the bottle and the

> 'I agree with Richard Raffan when he said that no matter how good the pattern or beautiful the wood, form is the only lasting thing.'

Photo 4 The breakline of the bottle should be in line with the trued up end.

thickness of your cover to be, for instance, 5mm $\frac{3}{16}$", then draw a line 5mm $\frac{3}{16}$" outside your first line.

In the area of the curves you may have to improve the shape a little. Cut out the two templates and you are ready to proceed. Now, for extra safety, measure L1 and L2 (FIG 1) on your inner template. To find the bottle's breakline, place a ruled set square next to it as in Photo 2.

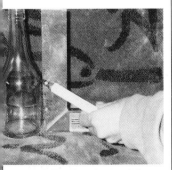

Photo 2 Finding the bottle's breakline.

Prepare your two pieces of wood. The section of each piece should be square and about the same. Mark the centre point in

both ends of the pieces (Photo 3).

Turning starts with the bottom piece. Mount it on a screwchuck, making sure you get the screw in the centre. (The screw should have parallel threads.)

The wood must, of course, be slightly longer than the lower part of the bottle, below the joint. There must be room for the screw and for the later off-cut.

I often glue waste hardwood in the bottom of the piece for a good grip of the screw. You must be able to remount the piece a couple of times.

Alternatively, you can use a

Photo 3 Mark the centres in both ends.

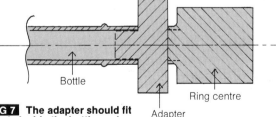

Bottle

Ring centre

FIG 7 The adapter should fit snugly inside the bottle neck.

Adapter

case. This is very important, because the wood must have a chance to move a bit without touching the glass.

Now fix the bottle in the centre of the recess, gluing it in the bottom (and only in the bottom) with a good flexible glue such as silicone.

You can centre the bottle exactly in the following way. Turn an adapter from a bit of waste hardwood. This should fit snugly inside the bottle neck and have a flat outer surface (FIG 7).

Place the bottle in place and use your toolrest to help you ▶

find the centre. Move the toolrest as close to the bottle's neck (the wider ring if there is one) as you can.

Now move the tailstock and its ring centre (with centre point removed if possible) towards the adapter and clamp lightly to it. Turn the whole piece by hand and move the bottle and the adapter until the bottle is perfectly centred. Clamp it with the tailstock and leave it overnight (Photo 5).

Photo 5 Clamp it with the tailstock.

If you want to go on with the other half at once, you can fix the bottle in place with a couple of thin sticks between it and the recess. Use long sticks so you can remove them later.

To mount the top piece you can either screw a faceplate to it or use another kind of chuck. Use long sheet screws (self-tapping) which have parallel threads.

Vibration will be reduced if the piece is mounted on a faceplate, especially if you're going to make the recess in endgrain. The recess is made in a similar way as for the bottom piece. You can do it all with turning tools, but there is a trick you can use.

As I mentioned, a bottle often has a wider ring just below the threads. Measure its diameter with callipers and alter your adjustable drilling bit to this.

Mount the piece in the top end and the drilling bit in a Jacobs chuck in the tailstock (Photo 6). Bore a hole through the piece, ensuring you don't hit the screw, or you may

Photo 6 Bore a hole through the piece.

destroy both drilling bit and screw.

It is very important that this hole should be perfect in size. Not so small that you can't get the bottle neck in, but not so wide as to leave a gap between this and the wood. The neck is the only part, except for the glued bottom, where bottle and case are in contact.

Continue to turn the recess with the help of your template (Photo 7). Note that the distance

Photo 7 Continue turning the recess, using your template as a guide.

between the bottle and the wood can now be more than 2mm $\frac{3}{32}$″ in the upper part (below the ring) due to the previous drilling.

Keep this in mind when you are turning the final outer curve, so the wood won't be too thin just here. In that case you will have to make the neck a little wider here.

When you are satisfied with the result, push the two pieces together to check the fit (Photo 8). If it's OK, align the

Photo 8 Push the two pieces together to check the fit.

grain, if necessary, and glue the pieces together.

Here are some tips you may need to do this.

● See that as little glue as possible comes into the space between bottle and cover. Wax the bottle near the joint so the glue doesn't stick to the glass.

● Don't remove the top

piece from its mounting, or the chuck from the driving centre.

● Use the tailstock as a clamp. You can use the screw-hole in the bottom piece for centre finding. Use the centre point in your centring (Photo 9).

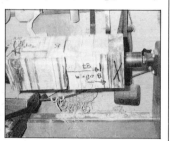

Photo 9 Again, use the tailstock as a clamp.

● Mark the place of the joint, so you know where it is later.

● Leave it overnight in the lathe.

● Put the piece aside awhile to let the water from the glue (if you have used a water-based glue) dry out from the wood. Otherwise, you can have unwanted movement in the finished piece.

Before you start the outer curve turning, I should point out that any scraping action must be avoided, or the thin cover will almost certainly be ripped out and destroyed. Use only cutting tools and actions.

Cut the crisp edges with a bandsaw, making the wood hexagonal if you want. Mount it on the lathe between centres, the bottom towards the head-stock, using a screwchuck instead of a driving centre (Photo 10).

Photo 10 Mount the trimmed wood on the lathe.

Make a note to remind you where the breakline is located. Turn it round and roughly make the shape. Leave at least 10mm $\frac{3}{8}$″ thickness everywhere at this time (Photos 11 and 12).

Photos 11 and 12 Turn the case round and shape.

Now locate the top of the bottle (L2 from breakline/joint) and carefully cut down until you hit the glass bottle just below the top. This is critical, so take it easy.

When you've done this, stop the lathe and remove the piece of wood to the right of the top.

Now mount your adapter in the bottle neck. Move the tailstock and clamp the ring centre gently to the adapter. Use the toolrest to check if the bottle neck is centred. If it isn't, it will end up looking like FIG 8 from above.

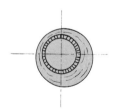

FIG 8 The bottle must be centred accurately or you will get an odd shape.

Do it like this. Loosen the piece slightly from the screw (a quarter of a turn will do) and then gently bend to the top of the piece and centre in the way I mentioned before.

This is why you should use a screw and not a faceplate in the bottom piece, as with a faceplate you can't make the necessary gentle bending.

Clamp in place with the ring centre and check again, using your adapter (Photo 13).

Photo 13 Check that it is centred.

Now turn the whole piece to its final shape with the help of your template, remembering the thickness of the neck. Take very light cuts, as too much force here and the piece could thread itself back to eccentricity (Photo 14).

Photo 14 Not too much force here.

The offcut at the top should be in the centre of 'the ring,' just below the threads. If you cut it off higher up, the bottle will be hopeless to pour from, while if you cut it lower there will be a space between the top of the bottle and the case.

Finish the turning with light cuts (again no scraping), but don't yet completely sever it at the bottom. Just cut halfway through, about 5mm ³⁄₁₆″ from the base of the bottle, making the offcut slightly concave. Now sand the piece.

Up to now the form, or design, of the cover has been decided by the chosen bottle. You can, of course, make some slight changes to improve the appearance, but there are limits.

In making the cap, however, you can either make or break the rest of the design. I agree with Richard Raffan when he said that no matter how good

Photo 15 A good bottle ruined by a bad cap.

the grain or beautiful the wood, form is the only lasting thing.

So don't just make any old cap, try to make one which is in harmony with the rest of the piece. Photo 15 shows a good bottle case destroyed by a bad cap.

If you decide on an *Edge to Edge* cap (FIG 9) you must be

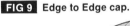
FIG 9 Edge to Edge cap.

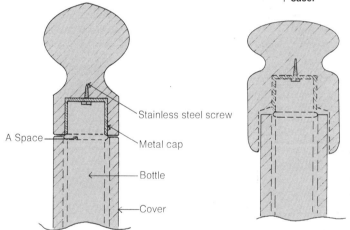

A Space
Stainless steel screw
Metal cap
Bottle
Cover

FIG 10 Outside cap.

Photos 16 and 17 Finish the cap.

careful to ensure that the gasket really comes into contact with the upper edge of the bottle. If it doesn't the bottle will leak.

On the other hand, the space at A shouldn't be too wide or it will ruin the appearance.

Turn the lower part of the wooden cap and make a recess for the metal or plastic screw cap. Make a jam fit chuck, mount the cap on it and finish the top (Photos 16 and 17).

Remove it from the chuck and glue the metal or plastic cap into the bottom of the recess (using epoxy glue) and secure it with a stainless steel screw in the centre.

To make an *Outside* cap (FIG 10), the space between the inner diameter of the cap and the outside diameter of the bottle should be about 1mm ³⁄₆₄″, so the two pieces can move about independently.

Cap

After finishing the cap, screw it on the bottle. Mount the whole piece on the lathe, check for fit, centre again (with the help of the tailstock, the toolrest and a soft pad between the ring centre and the top of the cap) and, if necessary, make light cuts to make the cap fit well (Photo 18).

Photo 18 Ensure the cap is a good fit.

Photo 19 The finished bottle case.

Now, the bottom can be completely cut off, the base sanded and, apart from finishing, the 'woodturner's bottle' is completed (Photo 19).

I often soak it with finishing oil several times over a long period before re-mounting on the lathe (friction mounting between centres) and wet sanding in finishing oil with a very fine grit.

If you want to give the bottle and case as a gift, tie a slice of endgrain to it as a tag with your friend's name and birthday burned in with a pyrography pen, and make a simple wooden box, lined with shavings. ■

You do not need to be able to use a skew chisel to be an effective spindle turner. I know of one well-respected turner who does not use one and manages perfectly well without, thank you. If however you are prepared to invest the time to learn how to use a skew, it will do the job of several other tools and to greater effect. It is the hardest tool to master and the most pleasing to use.

The main use of the skew is in spindle turning or in turning items such as boxes. It works best where the grain of the timber runs parallel to the axis of the lathe and is most commonly used on straight sides. It is also very useful for cutting across the grain as in the making of beads and coves, particularly if you adapt it as I suggest. The skew is not an efficient hollowing tool.

In all the uses I shall describe, the bevel should be hollow ground because, as in practically all turning tools, the cutting edge can be more accurately placed if you start your cut with the bevel rubbing. This is not possible with a convex bevel. The edge is sufficiently sharp straight from the grinding wheel but, if you do wish to use a stone to hone the edge, you will no doubt get a sharper tool. That sharpness will not last long enough however to warrant the effort involved.

The handles of skew chisels do not need to be thick or long as great leverages are not involved. Short handles have the great advantage of being much more manoeuvrable.

Many species of timber are suitable for spindle work, so selection can be based on factors such as appearance and ease of supply. It is best to avoid wild grain and burrs and, for practice, nothing is better than a small branch of a tree preferably still green. It will have the advantages of being free, not much use for anything else and vaguely round. I

SKEWS PLEASE

DAVE REGESTER

The author looks at the many ways in which the skew chisel can be used to advantage.

Dave Regester has been turning professionally since 1974. In his workshop in Tiverton, Devon, he makes salad bowls, scoops and platters, which he sells through high-class kitchenware shops, and one-off pieces, which he sells through galleries and exhibitions.

advise you to concentrate on mastering the tool rather than making anything, apart from shavings and mistakes.

With the grain running parallel to the axis of the lathe, all cuts are made from the largest diameter to the smallest so that the fibres you are cutting are supported by the uncut fibres beneath them. If you go uphill you will not get a smooth finish (you may not even finish at all).

Since most spindle work is of a small diameter, the lathe speed can be quite high. But, when you are practising a new cut or using a new tool, it is a good idea to start at a slow speed and increase it as you gain confidence.

As you will see from the photos, my skews have curved edges. This is not only because nature abhors a straight line but that they cut better that way. I recommend you sharpen one of your skews that way and see if it works for you. Some of the cuts I do with a curved skew cannot be done with a straight edge and other cuts are just made easier. It also increases the range of angles to which you can align your tool to the work. I think the only reason why skews are supplied with a straight edge is that it is easier for manufacturers to sharpen them this way. You should never be frightened to alter a tool so that it works better for you.

As you will know, the piece of metal the tool is made from has four faces, two are narrow and two are wide. In some cuts the wide face is supported on the tool rest and in some it is the narrow. In the case of curved cuts however the tool is rolled from one face to the other. This is why it is a good thing for the tool to be made from a piece of steel that is oval in cross-section as in the case of Sorby's. If your tool is more traditionally made, you can achieve the same effect by grinding off the sharp angles.

A further adaptation of the tool

is to soften the sharp angles where the bevel meets the flat surface of the tool. This is particularly desirable at either extremity where, especially when cutting coves, there is a risk of marks being left on the work. Sorby's new design overcomes the need for this.

I shall now describe some of the different ways in which the skew chisel can be used.

Planing Cut

This is the commonest mode and can be used to convert square stock to a smooth cylinder. I prefer to use a roughing gouge to remove the square edges so that I keep my skew sharp. But in the case of small diameter work, I use a skew for the whole operation.

The rest is positioned as close to the work as possible but always rotate the work by hand before starting the lathe to ensure it does not snag the work. The rest should be approximately the same height as the centre of the work and the tool should operate on the quadrant between the rest and the top of the work.

For obvious reasons, the sharpest point of the skew is called the toe and the other end of the edge the heel. The planing cut is one of the cuts that is done by the edge between heel and toe rather than the point. Many people do the cut with the heel pointing downwards (Photo 1). This is

1 Traditional way of using skew

the way that Richard Raffan was taught. It was only when he met someone who had not been taught how to use the skew and was using it the wrong way that he discovered it is in fact the best way (Photo 2). I am indebted to Richard for passing this on to me.

2 The 'wrong' way

It is easier to demonstrate the advantages of using the skew point downwards than to describe it. The angle of the edge to the work can be the same either way. But as you can see from the photos, in order to get (1) cutting at the same angle as (2) the tool needs to be at the right angles to the work. Since the force of the cut is along the axis, this means that the left hand and the right need to be pushing sideways on the tool. In (2) the force is along the tool and is mostly supplied by the right hand with the tool being an extension of the forearm. Not only is this easier but, because the left hand is more or less redundant, it can be taken off the tool and used to support the

work to stop it whipping or to catch it when parting off.

When first trying this cut, start with a cylinder of wood between centres and start the lathe at a slow speed. Hold the tool as shown in photo (2) at one end of the work. Make the bevel rub the work and gradually ease the handle away from the work so that the tool starts to bite. As it bites, push the tool in the direction of the cut, maintaining the angle between the work and the tool. With practice you will be able to present the tool at the correct angle without rubbing the bevel first.

The function of the hand on the rest is not to hold the tool onto the rest as is sometimes supposed. The force exerted by the rotation of the work onto the tool does this, the hand at the rest is simply there to guide the tool in conjunction with the hand on the handle. Because the tool slides along the rest for a long distance on this cut, and because the angle of cut is so critical, it is important that the rest is smooth. **If there are any scars on the rest it is best to remove them with a file.**

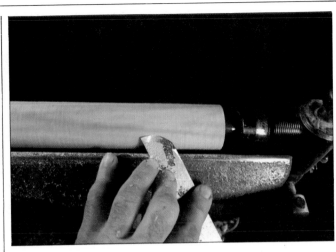

On a reasonably straight-grained piece of wood, you ought to be able to get a finish that requires little sanding, provided your tool is sharp. If you find that the grain tears, it may be because the angle between the axis and the edge is wrong or you are taking off too thick a cut, i.e. you have lifted the bevel too far from the work. If you still cannot get a smooth finish, try applying a little oil or water to the wood (choose one that is compatible with your finish). This should help the tool to cut the rough bit. Alternatively try a variant on

3 Variant of planing cut

the planing cut which is only possible with a curved edge. Hold the tool so that the edge is parallel to the axis (Photo 3) and the bevel rubbing. Lift the tool handle slightly so that the edge bites and, when you have found the angle to produce fine shavings, you can slide the tool along the work at that angle.

Peeling Cut

Sometimes you need to remove a large quantity of wood from the end of a cylinder, e.g. when forming a cylinder (Photo 4).

4 Peeling cut

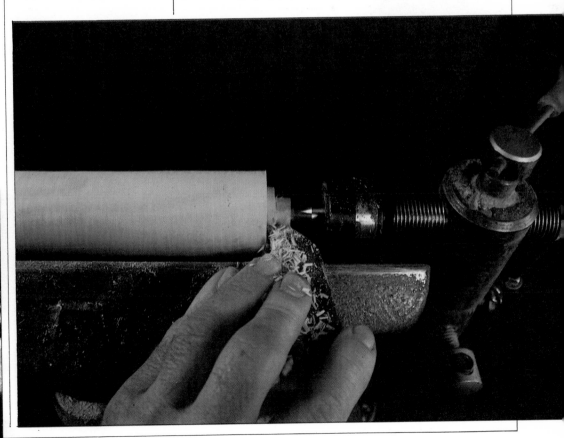

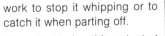

You can use a straight chisel to do this or you can use a skew, the principle is the same. The tool is held at right angles to the axis, its widest face flat on the rest. You will not be able to take a very wide cut because it will exert more force on the work than the driving centre can impart without drilling a hole in the end of the timber. Aim to take a cue 3mm ⅛" wide, rest the bevel on the work, raise the handle end and push upwards into the work. The progress of the edge from outside to centre describes an arc when viewed from the end (Photo 5).

5 Peeling cut

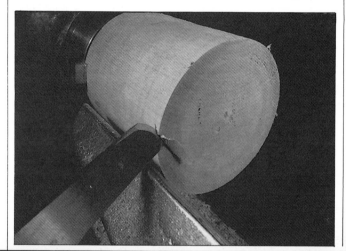

Slicing Cut

This cut describes the same arc as the peeling cut but uses the point of the skew to clean off the end of a piece (Photo 6). The contact between the tool and the rest is on the narrow face of the tool and the bevel rubs behind the point so that

7 Catch on slicing cut

the tool subtends an angle to the axis exactly equal to the bevel. If you get this wrong, a catch results (Photo 7).

Some people recommend using the heel for the slicing cut but

8 Rounding off the end

this is much more difficult, partly because the point you are using is obscured by the rest of the tool — try it and see. On a good piece of wood, you will require no sanding after this cut.

To round off the end of a piece, you use the same cut with a rolling action of the wrist. Once the shape is achieved with the point, the surface can be given a final smooth cut with the part of the edge just back from the point (8).

With this array of techniques at your disposal, it is possible to make an enormous variety of articles with the skew chisel and its relation. I shall cover further modifications of the tool, and items to be made, in my next article (page 50). ∎

6 Slicing cut

In the third part of his mini-series on spindle or between centres turning, Chris Pye shows how to turn bedposts.

Make your own bedposts

Turners trying to make a living from the craft must produce good work quickly and efficiently, because they are paid by each item made.

To do this they need to cut 'down time', (which I describe on page 9 in this mini series) and also something

Photo 1 A fat column like this causes tools to overhang the toolrest.

else which I call (for want of a better word) 'unproductive time'.

This is time even less connected with the job in hand. It includes getting in late, answering the phone, chatting to customers, brewing up, being distracted by other interests and so on.

Not that these activities aren't necessary, but they don't contribute directly to what makes the money – turning the wood.

Seeing a customer is important, and you must be polite and welcoming, but you can't afford to chat for an

hour about something in the news.

If you find you're not producing much at the end of the day it's worth doing a bit of the old 'time and motion' to see how you are spending the time.

It is not much good in the long term turning out a table leg in one minute if you spend the next 10 not turning anything. And this applies not only to spindle turners of course.

It's common for many would-be professional turners to fritter away time unproductively, all of which time must be paid for by the

productive time.

In other words, if you are working for 40 hours in the week but spend half the time unproductively, then you'll have to double your prices to carry that 'dead' time in order to achieve what you would have made if you were working fully productively. This also means building into your costs sickness and holiday time.

No one works 100% productively, but taking the balance of productive and unproductive time into consideration will help pay the bills better.

Spindle turning for a living, as I

have said, covers much that is run of the mill, legs in units of four, for example. Some work is much more challenging – exceptionally wide or long (Photos 1 and 2).

The bedposts I'll describe how to make here are some 2590mm 102" long. Some posts are even longer. My lathe will handle up to 2895mm 114".

Wide pieces create the problem of tools overhanging the toolrest, which means having to adjust it. Slender pieces have the problem of whipping, which I discuss on page 69.

The bedposts

My bedposts (FIG 1) needed to be turned in parts because the long centre section (the 'stem') had to be fluted separately. So the main problem was how to accurately join these fairly large pieces of wood together, boring the hole truly in line and marrying the pin or spigot neatly to it.

When wood is turned between centres, any cylinder created will naturally fall in line with the axis. I experience little difficulty in making the spigot in line with the axis, though getting it a true cylinder at the right diameter needs care. The problem is in boring the hole.

The normal practice is to bore a hole with a chuck in the mandrel, in place of the drive centre, pushing the wood into it by winding in the tailstock. This is far safer than having the wood revolving on the drill bit.

Many turners have Forstner bits, which have a wide application in turning, and use them to bore holes in the ends of posts to take spigots.

This is understandable, as the hole needed is quite large (at least a third the diameter of the post) and the bits are easily available for mounting in a standard chuck.

But I discovered early on that, although Forstner bits have many uses, they are often unsuitable for boring holes in post ends.

The reason is that, as they cut the hole, the wood of the post hangs on the side of the cutting bit as it is cutting and the weight eases the bit off course (FIG 2).

FIG 1 The bedpost is made in three parts needing two strong joints. If the middle section was not fluted, this post could have been made in one piece.

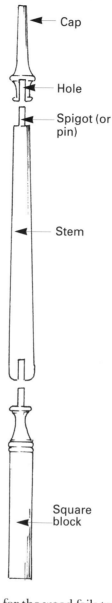

Cap

Hole

Spigot (or pin)

Stem

Square block

Using a support for the wood fails to solve the problem of a large bit drifting off the axial line, resulting in the spigot entering askew. Even the slightest non-

Photo 2 The main problem with these long, fat newel posts, was working between the square sections.

Photo 3 A twist bit with Morse taper and pilot end, and the pilot drill bit that leads the main bit. The smaller bit may be used to guide the pilot.

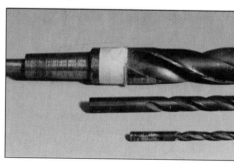

alignment is unacceptable here.

My solution to the problem was to find a twist bit of the size I wanted, and with the appropriate Morse taper to fit my lathe. A twist bit supports the wood all the way along and will always run true.

Engineering suppliers have such bits readily available to fit engineering lathes. I got an engineering firm to turn down the bit's leading 25mm 1" to a 12mm ½" DIA (Photo 3). This leading part follows a pre-drilled pilot ▶

FIG 2 A Forstner bit will tend to wander in this application, the longer the hole that is being bored the more evident.

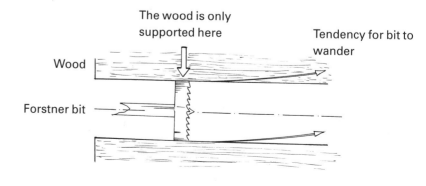

The wood is only supported here

Tendency for bit to wander

Wood

Forstner bit

hole of the correct diameter 12mm ½".

Let's return for a moment to the start of the job. The wood must be accurately prepared, cut neatly to lengths and the centres precisely marked.

To join the three pieces of each post (top, middle stem, and base block) I needed two holes and two spigots.

I followed my earlier dictum of doing all the marking out together, all the boring in one go and turned the paired pieces of each post together, to reduce down time.

I used a supporting 'shelf' made from a normal wooden toolrest as a jig for the part of the post to be offered for boring (FIG 3).

I aligned the centre of the post in the jig first, using a pointed nail in the drill chuck (Photo 4). Once set up I could put in each piece knowing it would be bored exactly in the centre.

This is particularly important with the longest pieces, as I would need to be an orang – utan to monitor and

FIG 3 An advantage of a wooden toolrest is that it's easily adapted to other purposes, in this case a jig to centre the   post for the boring of the pilot hole.

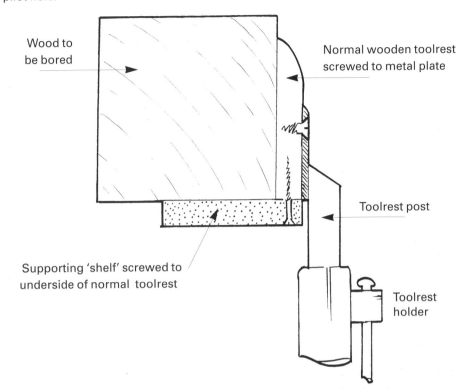

Wood to be bored

Normal wooden toolrest screwed to metal plate

Toolrest post

Supporting 'shelf' screwed to underside of normal toolrest

Toolrest holder

guide the boring end, while winding in the tailstock.

Before the 25mm ½" pilot hole, I often bore a smaller pilot. This makes the boring smooth, again important when I'm working on my own and can't be at both ends at once.

The large pilot (Photo 5) is followed by the main bit itself, mounted directly in the mandrel. It follows the pilot exactly and produces a dead straight smooth hole (Photos 6 and 7).

To turn the posts the holes need to be plugged. These I make with quite a slow taper. 10 DEG or so will grip well. To help the plugs seat accurately in the hole I mark them with a series of

Photo 4 Lining the centre of the post with the centre of the chuck (and therefore the mandrel).

Photo 5 Pilot drill first. Note the wood resting on the shelf fixed beneath the wooden toolrest.

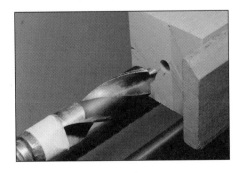

Photo 6 Main drill bit mounted in the mandrel of the lathe in place of the chuck and the reduced end about to follow the pilot hole.

Photo 7 Boring the main hole. With this method a high degree of accuracy is obtained.

rings (Photo 8) and tap them in up to a line.

When you need to dress the end of the post you will normally nick into the plug. It's important that you take up what is now slack in the plug by tightening the tailstock.

If the plug has gone into the hole too deep to be tapped out with a hammer a pipe-gripping wrench will easily twist it out (Photo 9).

The spigots, or pins, are made during the normal course of turning. Using the skew and a roughing gouge I come to within about 3mm ⅛" by eye.

I can do this because I know the diameter of my drive centre and take this as my reference. This avoids the use of callipers.

Because the toolrest is aligned along the lathe's axis I can use it as a fence for my fingers to get a true cylinder on the spigot. I also eye through to the bed of the lathe as a second check (Photo 10).

Next comes the sizing gauge, *set at a little over the finished size* (Photo 11). Finally I dress the surface with a broad chisel (Photo 12) and try the pin in the hole. Within a shave or two I should get a snug fit.

It's crucial for me to remember exactly what I did, and what sort of shaving I took, so I can repeat the actions and get to the exact size quicker.

An important point here: should you take an extra 1mm ³⁄₆₄" of shaving

Photo 9 If the plug has been pushed deeply in the hole, a pipe wrench will ease it out.

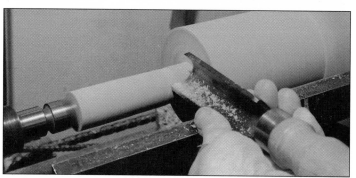

Photo 10 Coming down to approximate pin size using the drive centre diameter and the toolrest alignment as my guide.

Photo 11 Sizing in several places to slightly more than the finished diameter.

off, the diameter of the wood diminishes by *twice* this. For as the wood spins round you take it off both sides.

This is one of the main reasons why such joints fail – everything is fine up to the last shaving. So it's worth those extra few minutes to sneak up on the finished size.

Once you've cut it too far, the pin will be loose and there's nothing you can do but wrap the joint in glued paper, never a happy thing.

The final join should be neat and strong, and rendered invisible by placing it in a natural groove in the design (Photo 13). The flat shoulders of the joint are dished very slightly to give a tight join.

The rest of the turning is straight- ▶

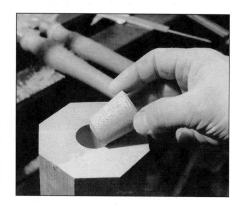

Photo 8 Plugging the hole. Note the lines scored in the plug to help align it in the hole so the post revolves centrally on the lathe.

Photo 12 A wide flat chisel trues and neatens the pin.I always go 'softly softly' on the last part, trying the pin for a snug fit, rather than risk it being loose.

Photo 13 The join is hidden as part of the design.

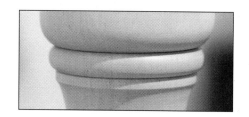

FIG 4 The toolrest can be used as a fence to guide the hands in cutting a tapered post.

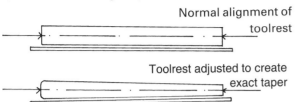

Normal alignment of toolrest

Toolrest adjusted to create exact taper

Photo 14 The top cap of the bed post, turned in the normal manner using the whole length of the toolrest.

Photo 15 The toolrest aligned for turning the stem of the bedpost.

forward (Photo 14) and features many of the characteristics of the spindle turning seen in the previous two articles.

For example, I set the toolrest and don't move it, do as much work with one tool before changing to another, use as few tools as possible and do minimal callipering.

Two more points are worth mentioning.

For the long stem I used a toolrest along the whole length, my normal practice (Photo 15), and turned a cylinder. The stem of the post tapers in an exact straight line. The stem will be fluted later.

I turned the taper as well as I could, by eye, on both stems and then adjusted the toolrest so it was aligned along the finished taper I wanted (FIG 4).

Using the toolrest in this position I could now run the roughing gouge and then the skew chisel to obtain the exact taper.

The trick is to keep the fingers and tools in the same position as you move your body smoothly along from one end to the other. You should work here, as with all turning, from the hips. The tapers can be matched well with this method.

Secondly, I try to cut the wood cleanly and precisely. In this case I was able to start the sanding at 240 grit. This not only saves time, but saves a lot of sanding, my least favourite job.

It's important to be aware of the level to which a finished piece needs to be sanded. These posts were to be French polished, so a fine finish was required.

But a pine newel post, which will be painted, might need only 120 grit, even 80, and it would be wasting time

Photo 16 The finished posts assembled for inspection. Note the different lengths of toolrest hanging on the wall.

to do more than is necessary.

Lastly, when I've finished the various parts I assemble the post and stand back for a critical inspection (Photo 16). It may be, because I'm working from a small picture rather than a working drawing (and a section at a time), that what looked good as a part doesn't work so well in the whole.

Sometimes I have to adjust the shape by returning the work to the lathe. The few extra minutes make a lot of difference to both my, and the customer's, satisfaction.

On this size of wood there's little vibration or whip. Slender, more truly 'spindly' work, has its own problems, and I'll look at this next time (p. 69). ∎

The author

Chris Pye has been both a professional woodturner and carver over some 16 years. He started with carving, owing his formative introduction to the master woodcarver Gino Masero, and a little later added woodturning.

He considers himself self taught, and equally at home in both crafts, often combining them.

Chris was born in Co. Durham but has lived a large part of his life in the South West of England. He has several years' experience teaching adult education classes in woodcarving as well as private students in both turning and carving. In 1991 he demonstrated at the AWGB Seminar at Loughborough.

His first book, *Woodcarving Tools, Materials and Equipment* was published by GMC Publications last year.

Chris Pye,
The Poplars,
Ewyas Harold,
Hereford HR2 0HU.

Dave Regester has been turning professionally since 1974. In his workshop in Tiverton, Devon, he makes salad bowls, scoops and platters, which he sells through high-class kitchenware shops, and one-off pieces, which he sells through galleries and exhibitions.

In my previous article (p. 42) I describe the basics of skew technique. With a little practice you can now make any number of useful objects some of which are so straightforward that all you need is the wood and the idea. Items such as rolling pins, honey dippers, light pulls, can now flow off the production line as fast as you can manage.

Cheeseboard Handles

One of the mainstays of my range for many years now is the cheeseboard with wire attached. This involves the making of handles to grip the wire with and, while they are not at all difficult to make, I have included two photos of stages in their production to illustrate how useful it is to be able to use the skew in either hand. (Photos no 1 and 2)

When I first started to turn the handles I found it very hard to make both sides equal because I would make the right hand side first, with my eyes over the centre of the handle, and then move a pace to the left to make the left-hand side. This meant I was looking at the left side of the handle with my eyes over the left hand end while trying to match a shape to my right. This is very difficult to do and is glorified by the technical name of parallax error.

More on the Skew

DAVE REGESTER

Cheeseboard handles, a child's rattle, lace bobbins – these are some of the favourite things the author shows you how to make with a skew.

If you can use the skew in both hands you can stand in the same position to cut both sides of an equal-sided object. This means that your eyes remain in the same position and you are able to make both sides the same.

There are two other advantages. One, you are able to examine very carefully your technique with your best hand when copying it with your worst hand. (It is always a good exercise to be self critical.) Two, you distribute the stress implicit in repetitive activity more evenly. In other words, you reduce the risk of suffering damage to your tendons.

1. Cheeseboard handle left side

2. Cheeseboard handle right side

Child's Rattle

One of the most interesting ornamental touches to a piece of spindle turning is the loose ring and the most practical use of this is in the child's rattle. I can lay claim, with perfect honesty, to having invented this object. I was asked to make a rattle and this was how I made a piece of wood rattle. I subsequently found out that such things are traditional (see Pinto's book on Treen). It's awfully hard to be truly original.

The stock used for the rattle is ash, but cherry and sycamore are equally good. For the good of the child, avoid splintery woods or poisonous ones. Always go for straight grain; it is a waste of exciting wood if used for something that is going to be put into the mouth and then thrown in the mud. I use 40mm 1½″ x 40mm 1½″ x 140mm 5½″ stock. It has to be small enough for a baby to hold without being so small that it can choke on it.

I am sure you do not need to be told how to get to photo 3. The narrow section to the right is the handle and the first ring is created using the toe of the skew with the tool well over on its side. You roll the tool over in a continuous flowing movement carrying the point downwards and into the face of the ring to create an overhang. Enlarge the vee cut to the right of this to enable the point to get right into the underhang and then work on the other side of the ring.

If you do your cuts in a smooth flowing movement you should get a smooth face to the ring but, before you break through, you should touch up the surface with a bit of fine grit paper. If you leave a large gap between the rings you can cut the ring free using your skew. But, if you like to make your rings as close together as possible, I recommend that you modify a skew chisel so that it has only one bevel as in photo 6. This enables you to get into a smaller gap but it is a tool that has a smaller margin for error than an ordinary skew, so be careful.

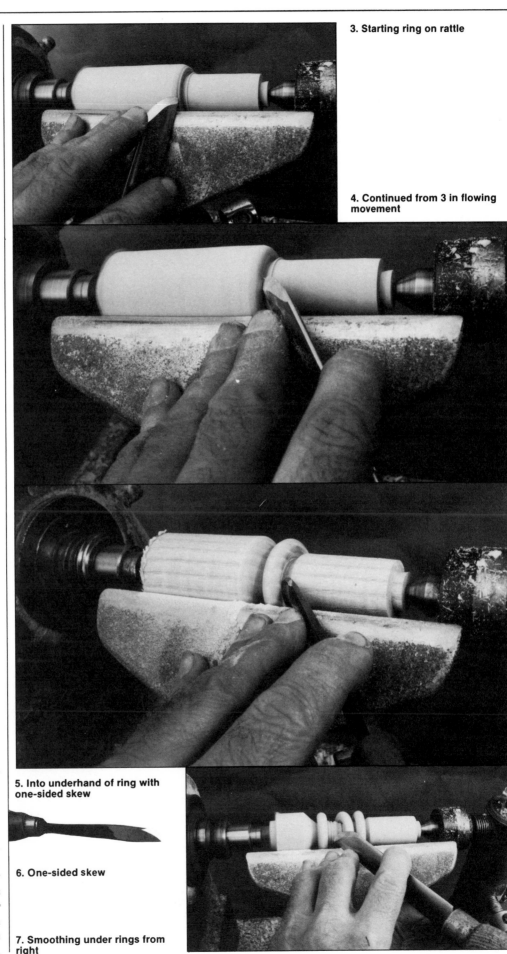

3. Starting ring on rattle

4. Continued from 3 in flowing movement

5. Into underhand of ring with one-sided skew

6. One-sided skew

7. Smoothing under rings from right

When you have separated as many rings as you like you can smooth the central rod as in photos 7 and 8. Once the diameter of the rod is small enough to enable the rings to move freely, you can hold them to one side to complete the finishing process (photo 9).

It only remains to form the handle. This shape (photo 10) is designed to echo the shape of the body. But, apart from aesthetics, the main criteria for the shape are the size of the user's hand and the necessity to avoid sharp edges.

I part off (photo 11) using the skew so that the end is smooth enough not to need any more finishing. I support the work in my left hand and leave as small a spigot as is necessary to support the rattle while doing a similar operation on the other end.

8. Smoothing under rings from left

9. Moving rings aside to finish underneath them

10. Finished rattle before parting off

11. Parting off rattle

Lace Bobbins

My lace bobbins are in many ways miniaturised rattles but they have some important differences. Before you make bobbins I strongly recommend you discuss their design with a lace maker, if you haven't the time or inclination to learn lacemaking yourself. There are several different types of lace and many different lacemakers, so you are never going to please everyone. But most makers will agree that the the important parts to get right are the 'thistle' on the end which should be of a shape that will enable the user to loop the thread round while not having sharp edges that wear out the thread. The capacity of the spindle will vary with the type of thread; my design is more likely to be too long if anything.

You will notice that I have a special rest for lace bobbins (photo 12). It is made of hornbeam because I am not a metal worker but the main purpose of its design is to fit between the centres of the lathe as closely to the work as possible. The advantage of having a special rest for one sort of object is, as you can see, that you can mark the rest with the dimensions. This means you do not have to stop to measure the length of each section. The only dimension I measure is the maximum thickness and one pre-set pair of calipers or a spanner takes care of that.

The stock for a lace bobbin must be of close and straight-grained wood because of the fineness of the spindle. There are plenty of native grown hardwoods that fit this category — such as laburnum (as illustrated), boxwood, yew, oak, rhododendron, spindle and so on — without exploiting rainforests. The size is 10mm ⅜″ x 10mm x 150mm 6″ and it is held in a 13mm ½″ chuck. This chuck only has 3 jaws but it seems to work on square-section stock when it is this small.

If you feel happier using round-section stock in 3 jaws, while you are finishing the bobbin, it

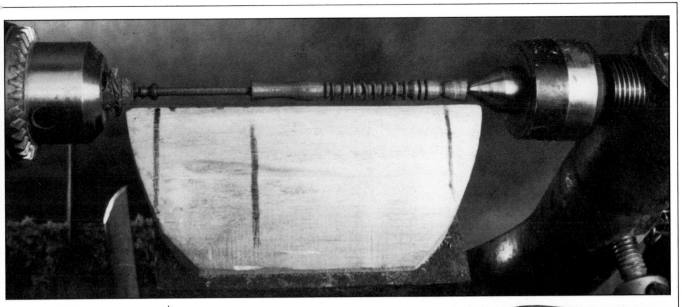

12. Lace bobbin

13. Modified skew chisel for small rings

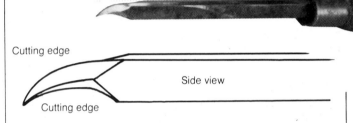

Cutting edge

Side view

Cutting edge

is easy to hold the square-section stock in the 3-jaws to round off one end and then reverse the stock so that this round end is then held in the jaws.

It is very useful to have a rotating dead centre for small work since any over-heating that you would get with a fixed centre could easily cause the work to discolour or split.

I like to make the bottom end of the bobbin fancy because this not only means that I can charge more for them but they are also readily indentifiable. I do this by means of rings either like those on the rattle or, as in this case, with an intervening ridge.

You obviously cannot get a 13mm ½" skew into the gap under the ring and even the one-sided skew is a little too thick. I have therefore modified the skew even further to produce a very fine point on the end of a sickle shape which has a bevel on both sides (photo 13). This was simply ground from square-sectioned tool steel and modified until it worked for me. Beware of slavishly copying this or any other tool until you really feel the need, have mastered the tool it is a modification of, and thoroughly understand the purpose.

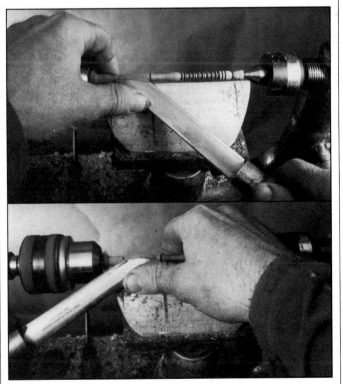

The fact that the work is gripped in the chuck means that there is no pressure exerted between the centres; it is nevertheless essential to support the work while it is rotating with the hand that is not holding the tool

(photos 14 and 15). This is in many ways the trickiest part of the operation since to make a mistake now would be a disaster, after you have already done so much work, and this is the finest part.

Photo 16 shows that the way the stock is held enables you to completely finish the end of the bobbin while it is on the lathe and, by supporting the bobbin with your hand, you can also finish off the thistle end.

I think if you can make a lace bobbin with rings on you can make practically anything between centres. Next stop Trunnion Boxes! (Page 64.) ■

14. Forming spindle cutting from right

15. Cutting spindle from left

16. Final parting off lace bobbin

PROJECT

P

JOHN FISHER

When John Fisher's wife took up bobbin-lace making, he decided he had two options – either to take out a second mortgage or learn to make bobbins.
The second option seemed more attractive. Initially, it was quite exciting too. He was using a dangerous combination of an electric drill, G-clamps and a vice .
Some 10 years later, he is still making bobbins, at his home in Hitchin, Herts, but much more safely and on a semi-professional basis.

Lace bobbins are satisfying to turn, provided you have an outlet for them. Almost any spindle-turning technique can be used, the main proviso being the product should be clean and smooth. So leaving bark on or using a blow torch is usually out.

I normally turn fairly simple bobbin shapes and let the wood provide the decoration. One type I hadn't made, until recently, was the mother-and-babe.

This is a traditional style, consisting of a normal East-Midlands bobbin (the 'mother') with windows cut into the body of the bobbin and a miniature bobbin (the 'babe') inserted into the space.

Bobbin A in the photo is an antique mother-and-babe. Like most of the best antique bobbins it is made of bone. My wife bought it for £6.50 from a bric-a-brac stall. Subsequently, we found that it was probably worth about ten times that amount.

It's still possible, of course, to make bobbins from bone, but I don't like the smell.

Bobbin B in the same photo, is another mother-and-babe, much less valuable, but one of my favourites. Again it's old, though probably not as old as Bobbin A.

It appears to have been whittled and is rather crude. However, some letters have been cut into it which points to the origin of decorating bobbins in this country.

They were presumably love tokens, whereas bobbins made by the so-called romantic Continentals are mostly plain, though the style may vary from area to area.

THE TECHNIQUE

As I say, I had never made a mother-and-babe. Then I read

John describes how to make a mother-and-babe bobbin.

Baby
bobbins

FIG 1

FIG 2

FIG 3

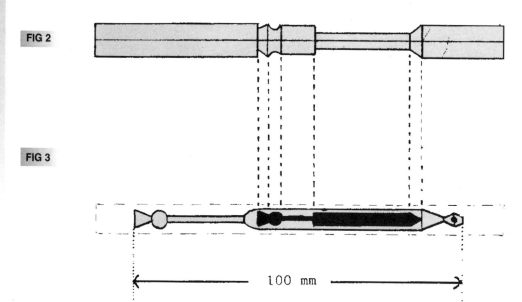

100 mm

'My wife bought a bobbin for £6.50 from a bric-a-brac stall. Subsequently, we found it was probably worth about ten times that amount.'

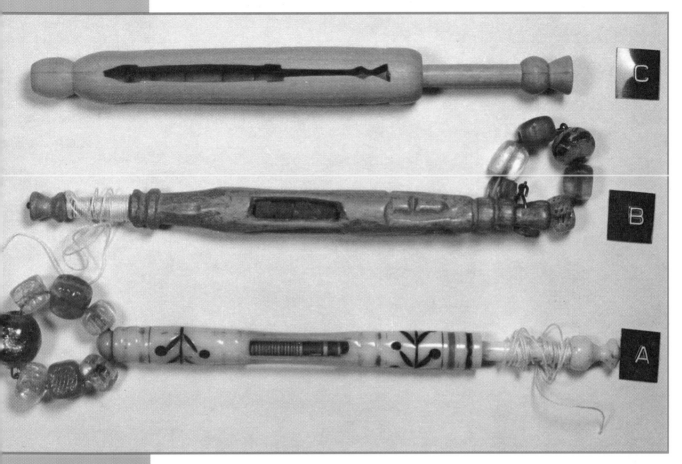

An antique bobbin (A), an old hand-carved bobbin (B), and a mother-and-babe bobbin (C).

Tobias Kaye's article in *Woodturning* (Issue 11). He saw his technique only being used for large projects, finials and so on, but it was so intriguing I wanted to use it for a bobbin and after producing much scrap now have some mother-and-babes for sale.

My method was as follows. For each bobbin I prepared four pieces of wood which when finished measured 5mm x 5mm x 125mm ³⁄₁₆" x ³⁄₁₆" x 5". So far I have used only one type of wood per bobbin, but the pieces could be of different woods.

They were bound with sticky tape to form a blank, FIG 1, and mounted on the lathe.

A 50mm 2" length of this was turned to the shape shown in FIG 2 and waxed (my usual finish).

Conventionally, the sides of the windows of a mother and babe are straight. However, I have taken advantage of this technique to make the window bobbin shaped.

The sticky tape was removed and the four pieces re-assembled (using Cascamite) with the previously turned sections on the inside of the new blank. Then the bobbin was given its final shape on the lathe.

I first worked the tail of the bobbin, at the tailstock end. Then the headstock end was turned to the maximum true cylinder.

This gives you a guide as to how far the cut-out section of the blank needs to be turned. Turning the cut-out section is,

of course, the tricky bit. I used light cuts with a skew chisel.

If the bobbin survived this far, I then turned it's head end, waxing as before. This gave a bobbin as in FIG 3.

Here only a basic-shaped window is shown but variations are possible. The babes were made from contrasting woods and sprung into the mothers.

Bobbin C in the photo is one of the bobbins made, consisting of a pequia 'mother' and a purpleheart 'babe'. Pequia is the yellowest of known timbers.

But mother-and-babes are not the only pregnant type of bobbin. Another traditional type is the cow-and-calf. Again it's an East-Midlands style. The spangle end of this 'cow' unscrews and out pops a small bobbin, the 'calf'.●

Bullseye

Ian French decided to combine his two loves – turning and darts – in one project and turned his own set of 'arrows'. He describes here how he went about it.

A s a turner with a passion for darts, I thought I'd combine my two loves and turn some dart barrels. The points and feather can be bought from a sports shop.

Many hours of experimenting and playing with shapes will be needed before you decide on the final design. The two I've chosen are very different, but equally effective (FIGS 1 and 2).

The first is fairly easy to make (Photo 1). To start, measure the diameter of the points you buy and the threaded part of the feathered flight stem.

Turn your timber – in this case lemon wood – to a cylinder and drill a hole in the end to the depth of the thread. A strip of tape around the drill

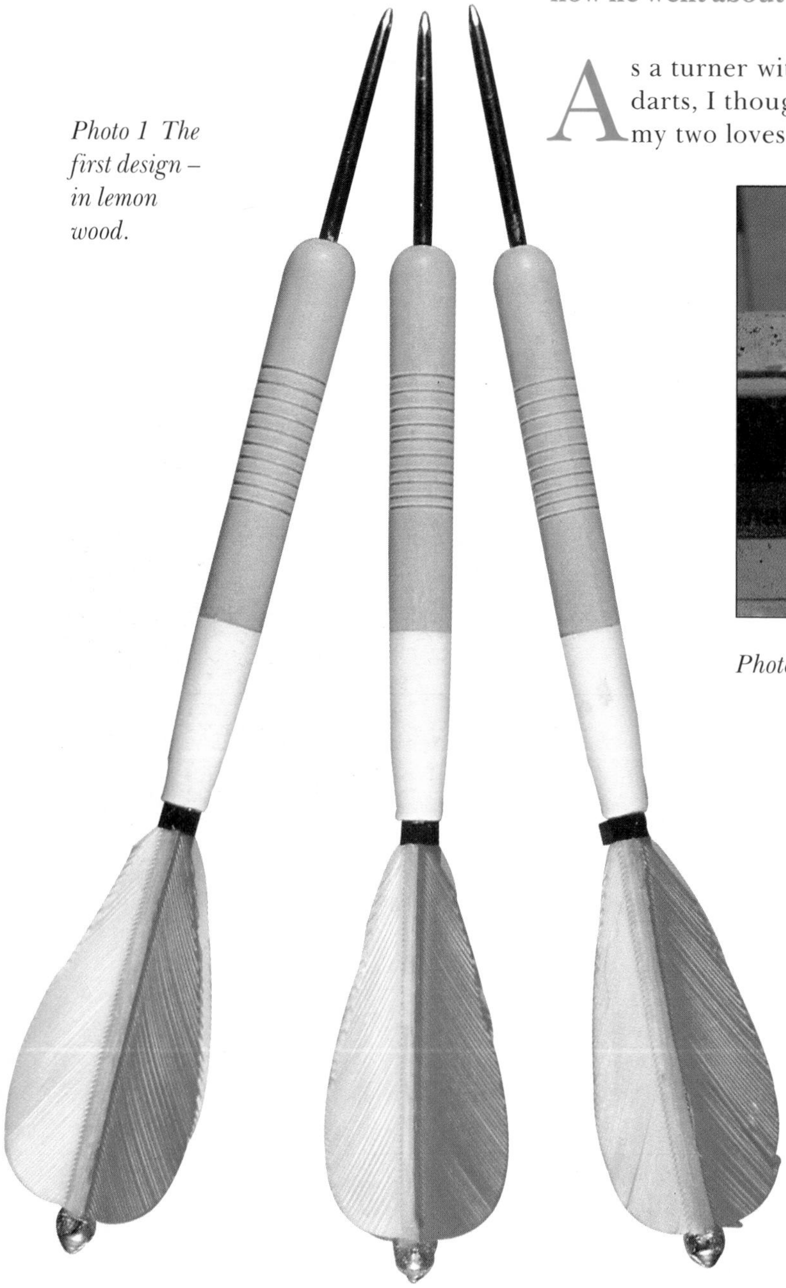

Photo 1 The first design – in lemon wood.

Photo 2 Turn your chosen wood to a cylinder.

Photo 3 Drill a hole in the 30mm 1 ⅛" pieces.

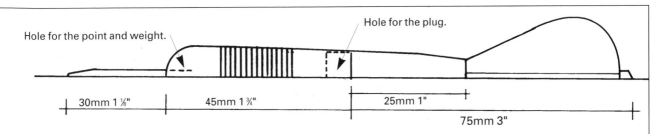

30mm 1⅛"   45mm 1¾"   25mm 1"

75mm 3"

Hole for the point and weight.

Hole for the plug.

FIG 1 My first dart – I only turned the 45mm 1¾" lemon wood barrel.

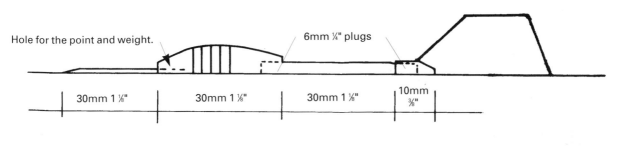

Hole for the point and weight.

6mm ¼" plugs

30mm 1⅛"   30mm 1⅛"   30mm 1⅛"   10mm ⅜"

FIG 2 My second dart.

will ensure your depth is right.

Cut the wood to the length you want the barrel to be and drill a hole in the other end for the point. The depth of this hole is up to you, depending on how heavy you want your dart. Obviously the deeper the hole, the more weight you can put in it.

Barrel

With a hole in each end, you will have to turn a plug to hold the barrel in the chuck. If you turn a shoulder on the plug to match the diameter of the stem, it will make shaping the barrel easier and ensure a flush fit.

You can now turn the barrel shape required. Turning V shaped grooves into the barrel will give you a better grip when throwing the dart. Sand and polish.

You're now ready to glue it all together. Glue the stem into your dart first. The thread will help bond it by giving grip. Now it's time for the point, and to weight your dart if you want to.

I suggest you melt-in some solder with a hot iron, leaving room to glue in the point once everything is set.

Photo 4 Also drill a hole in the other end of the barrel.

Clean off any excess glue and your darts are ready for use.

The second dart involves a lot more turning. Again, you can buy the flights and points. Or you can make your own point from a crochet hook, which will also leave some metal for weighting the dart. Measure the diameter of this hook before you start, as you'll need this information later on.

Darts are useful projects to make because you can turn them from off-cuts. I used turu and sycamore for my second set.

▶

Photos 5 and 6 Turn a plug – one end for the barrel and one for the top.

Photo 7 You should now have three pieces to glue together.

Whatever your wood, turn it to a cylinder (Photo 2) and cut to the barrel length you want, in this case 40mm 1 ⅝" (30mm 1 ⅛" for the barrel and 10mm ⅜" for the top).

There is no regulation length for a dart's barrel or stem, though manufacturers only make certain sizes and this unofficially governs length. The same is true with weights, but the companies make them of between 16 and 40 grammes.

Deeper hole

Into the 30mm 1 ⅛" section drill a 6mm ¼" hole of 3mm 1/8" DIA (Photo 3), or whatever the diameter of your point is. Again, a deeper hole can be used for weight.

You should also drill a 3mm ⅛" DIA hole in the other end of the barrel to take the 6mm deep plug. Mark with an X at the point end (Photo 4).

Into the 10mm ⅜" wood, drill a 6mm ¼" deep hole in one end. Take the rounded down sycamore and cut it to 42mm 1 ⅝", 6mm ¼" for each plug and 30mm 1 ⅛" for the stem.

On each end, turn a plug of 3mm ⅛"

*Photos 8 and 9
Don't apply too
much pressure
when turning,
because the joints
will be weak spots.*

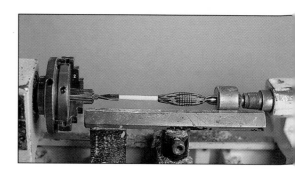

Many hours of experi-menting and playing with shapes will be needed before you decide on the final design.'

)IA and 6mm ¼" long to fit into the uru (Photos 5 and 6), one end for the barrel and the other for the top.

Glue

You should now have three pieces ready to glue together in the following order: turu (30mm 1 ⅛"), sycamore (42mm 1 ⅝") and turu (10mm ⅜"), as in Photo 7.

Ensure the barrel is the right way round for gluing, then bond with a wood glue, clamp and leave to dry.

Now it's time to turn your dart, using gauge and skew chisel (Photos 8 and 9), taking care not to apply too much pressure, as the joints will be a weak spot during turning.

When complete, sand and polish your dart (Photo 10). Do this sepa-rately if you have a light and dark wood together, as the colours may run during polishing.

Part off your dart (Photo 11) and ensure the top is flat, as this will help you in the next step.

You now have to cut a slot in the top of the stem (Photo 12) for the flight, using a coping or hack saw. Remember, the finer the blade, the tighter the fit.

If, when you fit the flight, it's still loose, stick it in place with strong glue (Photo 13). It's now simply a case of fixing in the point. If you want to weigh the dart, now is the time to do so.

Either fill most of the hole with sol-der, or cut some metal off the other end of the crochet hook handle. Make sure you leave room to glue in the point.

Grind the hook on your crochet hook to a point and glue in place with a strong glue, then leave to dry (Photo 14).

Clean off the excess glue and give the darts a trial throw. Who knows, you could hit a BULLSEYE. ■

The author

Born in Rugby, Warwickshire, in 1971, Ian French left school in 1988 and went to work for a woodturner. He enjoys the variety of the work.
Ian admires fine turned pieces, always looking for practicality as well as quality. Poor turning upsets and frustrates him. He feels this is an exciting time to be involved in woodturning.
His other interests include darts, snooker and cricket – much to the annoyance of his colleagues when there is a test match on the radio.
Ian still lives in Rugby.

Photo 10 When complete, sand and polish the dart.

Photo 11 Part off your dart.

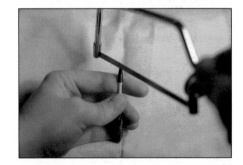

Photo 12 Cut a slot in the top of the stem to hold the flight.

Photo 13 If the flight is too loose, glue it in.

Photo 14 Glue your painted crochet hook in place with strong glue

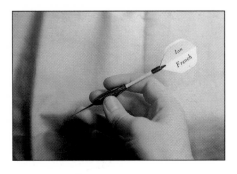

Photos 15 Give the darts a trial throw.

On 29 January 1991 I received a FAX from Bernard Cooper informing me that I first contacted him one year ago. I would like to take this opportunity to say that I really have enjoyed my first year of writing for *Woodturning* and feel privileged to be a member of the team. It has been a real high to work with Bernard Cooper — we FAX back and forth regularly and our correspondence is now a 2" thick file.

A wonderful thing the FAX. I do most of my writing in the evenings. I always finish a session by walking to our office, which is about 550' (167m) from our house, and taking advantage of the low international phone rates to FAX my story. After writing about long forgotten methods it is mind boggling to think that the story

Ernie Conover is our contributing editor in America. He teaches woodworking in general, and woodturning in particular, at Conover Workshops, a school he and his wife Susan operate together. In addition to writing and lecturing widely, he is a technical consultant to a number of companies on design and manufacture of woodworking tools and machines.

is instantly on Bernard's desk. Since the UK is five hours ahead of us, my FAX is waiting for him in the morning.

During our initial exchanges, Bernard gleaned that I was a co-founder of our woodworking

Turning a Flute Case

ERNIE CONOVER

There's much to be learned by making the case which Ernie and his daughter Genoa designed.

school. The Conover Workshops. Co-founder is close to Conover so, with his impish nature, this was quickly mutated to Co-founder, the handle I have been known by ever since. Now that

you know, I will sign my work for *Woodturning* as 'The Con-founder' and I like to think I confound you the reader a bit?

This issue I would like to outline the constructing of a flute case because it is a practical exercise building on my first two articles in *Woodturning*. We will turn the project using the chucking methods outlined in my first article and turn the knob for the lid from Tagua nut — covered in the second issue. Finally we will explore the grinding of a special scraper for turning the captive ring and cover an ancient but beautiful finishing method that can be done almost instantly in the lathe.

The design for this flute case is something my daughter Genoa and I cooked up to transport her recorder flute to school and back. Playing a recorder flute is part of our school's music programme, so everyone inherits one in third grade. I have constructed three recorder cases, but have been saved from a fourth because the school dropped the programme. Seeing as the flute is a $3 plastic gizmo, it is like putting a Hong Kong watch in a gold case.

The case I made for my eldest son Charlie was like Genoa's except that we made the whole case to imitate a recorder flute. The top was a crude whistle affair that resembled the mouthpiece of a recorder. We drilled some finger holes in the case itself so that the effect was a flute within a flute. Blowing on the lid/whistle produced a flute like sound that would cause our Labrador retriever to howl, but then Charlie's playing did that too.

For Genoa's case we went for straight function and design. The case is close fitting to the flute and has heavy walls to withstand the rigours of an itinerant student musician. The lid is a friction fit and has a vegetable ivory knob. The body has a node at each end and a captive ring between. Besides being a flamboyant show of the turner's art, the ring serves the practical purpose of retaining

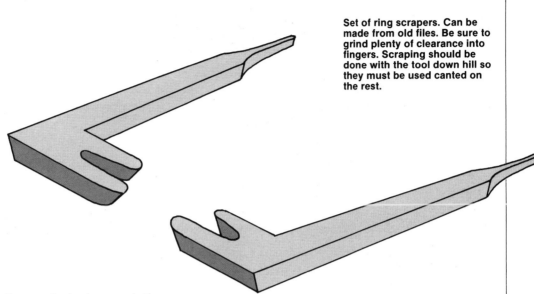

Set of ring scrapers. Can be made from old files. Be sure to grind plenty of clearance into fingers. Scraping should be done with the tool down hill so they must be used canted on the rest.

the music book around the case.

I started with a billet that was about 90mm 3½" square. I glued up stock for this from eight quarter cherry planks which were quarter sawn. Being a traditionalist, I used hide glue but any good wood glue is fine. Hide does have several advantages. Most turning can take place once the glue is jelled, usually about 15 minutes. The joint can be reversed easily in the first few hours with the application of heat and or water. Finally it does not affect finish if some is left on an exposed surface. Since the billet was to be drilled, I allowed the glue a full 24 hours. Once dry, I mounted the billet between centres and turned it to a perfect round and trimmed the ends square to just shy of the centres.

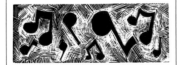

Chuck

Next I turned a chuck to accept the billet for drilling. This was simply a matter of scraping a cup-like pocket with a flat bottom and straight walls that were a slide fit with the round. I made the pocket about 38mm 1½" deep. I then brushed some hide glue on the round, slid it in

the cup and caught the centre mark with the tailstock. Once the glue jelled, the billet was held secure for drilling.

I did the drilling with a Forstner bit because it leaves a flat bottom and is much more immune from following grain. I had an old 35mm 1⅜" Forstner, gleaned from a flea market, with a square taper shank for use in a bit brace. For drilling this deep 340mm 13⅜" hole, I held the Forstner in an extension with the square taper shank cut off so that it could be held in a normal drill chuck in the tailstock. The old Forstners had almost no (some had none) brad point. Modern Forstners, designed for use in the drill press, have a much more pronounced point which makes them follow grain more readily. Shortening this point to just a stub makes a bit much more suited to straight drilling in the lathe.

The actual drilling was done with the lathe set to a low speed of 660 rpm. It is important to start the lathe before you start drilling to ensure perfect centring and to retract the bit from the work often to clear chips. Failing to clear often will result in the drill binding with disastrous results. This is important to remember in all drilling situations. I used the

actual recorder flute to inspect depth and allowed 12mm ½" extra for the fit of the cap.

Once drilled, I unscrewed the cup chuck from the face plate and placed it in a can of hot water to break the hide glue joint. While it was soaking, I mounted another billet end grain on the face plate and turned a gentle 38mm 1½" taper that bracketed the 35mm 1⅜" inside diameter of the case. I then went back to the billet and removed it from the chuck. I then slipped the open end over the freshly turned taper and caught the previously chucked end with the tailstock. I had the existing centre mark to pick up.

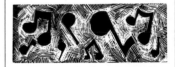

Scrapers

Next it was the captive ring and for this I had to grind a set of scrapers. While an old file is excellent for a scraper, some care should be exercised because a file is very hard (63° to 64° R_c scale) and can snap. They are fine for small scrapers that don't overhang the tool rest very far. For bigger scrapers I like pieces of old car spring.

Being spring temper they are just right for scrapers and can even be burnished (ticketed) the traditional way.

Files are just so tempting though, because they are readily available and shaped right to begin with. With a bit of blacksmithing there is a way we can alter the file to our needs. We need to start by annealing the file and the easiest way to do this is to place it in the coals of a strong burning fire in a fireplace or stove. Keep an eye on it and make sure the entire file becomes bright cherry red colour. It is best if you can just allow the fire to burn out and the file/s will cool slowly which is the idea here. If that is not possible fill a pail with some wood ashes, remove the incandescent file from the fire with tongs and plunge it into the wood ashes. Do not disturb it for a couple of hours. The ashes have a strong insulating quality and will cause the blank to cool slowly. When cool, your file should now be fully annealed — or in layman's terms, dead soft. An easy check is to file it with a good file — if it cuts easily it is soft.

Now is the time to do the rough shaping of the tool you intend to build. You can use a good file, bench grinder and abrasive belt machines to perform this task. I like to sand away all of the original file teeth leaving smooth metal that slides on the tool rest. Once you have the desired shape it is back to the fire, only this time just heat the tip where the cutting edge will be. For the average scraper this is usually about an inch or so. You want the tip a bright cherry red again and now instead of ashes, plunge it straight down into a bucket of water and instantly cool the blank. It is best to swish it around in the bucket vigorously to prevent steam build up around the blank. If everything goes right, the result is that the portion that was bright cherry red will now be file-hard again.

You can test this with the good file, it should skate on the hardened surface.

Tempering

To do the job properly you now want to draw the hardness back a bit from full hard — a process called tempering. To be able to judge the temper, it is necessary to polish the entire blank to a bright mirror-like finish. Now slowly and evenly heat the blank about an inch behind the cutting edge in a blue, colourless gas flame. An ordinary gas range or a propane plumber's torch is fine for this task. A gas welding torch tends to be too hot. Watch carefully and, as the temperature of the piece increases, colours will appear. Heat until the edge is straw colour. You can go as far as a blue spring temper (which is what you will have at the point you are running through the flame) and still be fine. If you go from a bright blue to a pale blue at the edge, however, you have gone too far and will have to redo the entire process starting with the fireplace. Once you see the proper colour, plunge the blank into the water again. Generally speaking cutting tools should be pale straw yellow (R_c 58-60°) or straw (R_c 55-58°) while scrapers and springs should be blue (R_c 45-50°).

The set of scrapers should be to the shape outlined in the drawing. I do most of the grinding with a bench grinder but I have a set of very thin wheels which are dressed to a radius for this type of work. A Dremmel TM tool, with a small abrasive wheel, may be useful if you lack thin wheels. The trick here is to have plenty of clearance everywhere and the uninitiated will find this a problem.

Body

I turned the outside of the case starting with the nodes at each end. I then roughed out the body working from both ends to the centre where I left the material for the ring. The work looked not unlike a culm of bamboo at this point. Now I shaped the outside of the ring by rolling a bead with a 12mm ½" spindle gouge. To separate the ring it was now a matter of alternately using the pair of scrapers, working gradually from each side. **Be sure to cant each scraper a bit on the rest to keep the end finger pointed down hill. This**

is very important if a catch is not to result. If one works carefully and gradually, the ring will drop off with just a small sharp edge to the inside. This can be easily smoothed by contact gluing a sheet of sandpaper around the case and starting the lathe while holding the ring. Sand the inside of the ring the same as if you owned an expensive spindle sander, which you do if you count your time for any value. **One word of caution is to make the ring of fairly heavy cross section for strength. Mine is 12mm ½" diameter finished.**

I then taped the ring to one side or the other with duck tape (2" wide aluminiumised tape used to tape heating ducks) to keep it out of the way. I finished the straight part of the case between the nodes with a skew chisel followed by 180 then 220 grit sandpaper. I now trimmed the tailstock end to a gentle radius ending just shy of centre. I later removed this centre nubbin with a chisel and cleaned it up with a bit of sandpaper.

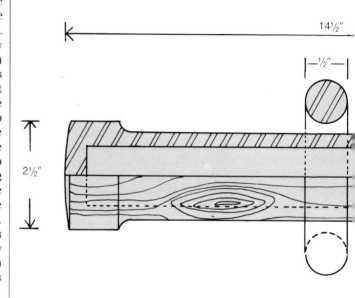

Finishing

I finished the case in the lathe with my favourite spindle turning finish — a French polish, turner style. To do this one needs real orange shellac made from shellac flakes. The canned variety has preservatives and extenders to give it shelf life which renders it unfit for French polish. I even like to make my shellac with grain alcohol. While my druggist knows me well enough to sell me what I need, it can be difficult to obtain pure grain alcohol. In a pinch I have used 200 proof grain alcohol sold in liquor stores here as Ever Clear. In America one usually finds Ever Clear stocked in a liquor store in a decidedly seedy section of town, the type that one would feel safer if one had a gun in one's pocket.

I mix my shellac in 200ml plastic camping bottles, by filling the bottle about ¼ full of shellac flakes and adding alcohol

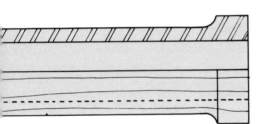

to just shy of the top. I shake the bottle well and again every hour or so until everything dissolves, then set it in direct sunlight for at least a day. A heavy sediment will fall to the bottom. I decant the liquid which is pure orange shellac. The sediment is a throwaway. An inexpensive brew for cleaning shellac out of brushes and equipment is a mixture of ammonia and water. It will even remove dried shellac and leave the brush good as new at a price much cheaper than denatured alcohol. To French polish in the lathe, apply a coat of shellac mixture

to the work with a full brush or a small bit of rag. I cut about 50mm 2″ squares of rag for lathe finishing and keep them on hand. If this small square is caught in revolving work it will not pull in your fingers with it, an important safety advantage over a whole rag. However you apply it, the critical point is to completely saturate the work. If a bit dribbles off that is OK. Remove the tool rest, stand aside and start the lathe. You need plenty of speed here — at least 1700 rpm. Grab a handful of shavings and apply them with lots of pressure to the revolving work. The shellac will melt under the burnishing action of the shavings leaving a pleasing French polish with none of the fuss, pumice, oil and other assorted trappings of conventional French polishing. It is important to turn the shavings often as they will become saturated with the excess shellac. French polish is a very thin finish. It is quite durable except to water which will leave a white mark. If marked, however, it is easily repaired.

To give the finish some water resistance and further beauty, I now apply some pure carnauba wax to the spinning work. It is difficult to find real carnauba wax. In its pure form, it is very hard like ice and shatters in the same way if dropped. Simply crayon some wax on the work and burnish with the shavings. The smell is that of a pipe shop as carnauba is the finish used on briar pipes. The results will be beautiful, with increased water resistance.

Cap

I now set about making the cap. I turned the cap in face plate orientation, which means the plank grain ran across the body of the case itself. More properly, for a lasting fit, it should have been spindle turned but the lid design would not have been structurally sound if turned in that orientation. I chose to use a bit of cork around the spigot of the cap to ensure a lasting fit. After Genoa's living with the case for several years now, I think the decision was a good one.

I turned the spigot and accompanying shoulder from a piece of cherry glued to a backing block on a face plate. After French polishing, I cut through the glue joint with a parting tool and jam chucked the freshly turned spigot. A bit of chalk in the chuck keeps the waxed part from slipping. It was then just a matter of turning and finishing the top of the lid and drilling a hole to accept the ivory nut knob. I drilled a 12mm ½″ hole for a spigot of the same diameter.

Knob

Finally I selected a large Tagua nut and set about turning the

knob. Turning was accomplished completely with a 6mm ¼″ spindle gouge. After turning I used a French curved cabinet scraper to remove the tool marks. It is easy simply to hand hold the scraper with no use of the tool rest. Then it was 180, 220, 320 and 400 grit sand papers followed by buffing with grey steel compound as described in my last article. I now scraped the spigot to 12mm ½″ and cut off. I glued the freshly turned knob into the hole in the cap and gave the case to Genoa for Christmas 1986. I might add that the instant quality of the French polish finish greatly aided my making the Christmas morning presentation.

Jam Chucking

In closing I would like to make another pitch for jam chucking.

I often find it is hard for people to grasp something if it is not eminently practical. We have put jam chucks to practical use in this exercise – in fact it would have been difficult to do the project otherwise. It is much too long for any of the spigot chucks. Yes, you could have used a three or four jaw engineering chuck, but an engineering chuck costs $250 plus and the protruding jaws present a real and ever present danger while turning. The jam chuck will never rap you on the knuckles and it costs nothing but your time. Only if you are a lawyer or a plumber will that approach $250.

Finally, the jam chuck is perfectly true to your lathe even if your spindle is not. With mechanical chucks you have the inaccuracy of the chuck plus or minus that of your spindle, depending if you are lucky or not. The jam chuck is dead nut accurate every time no matter what the run out of the spindle.

The Confounder ∎

Dave Regester has been turning professionally since 1974. In his workshop in Tiverton, Devon, he makes salad bowls, scoops and platters, which he sells through high-class kitchenware shops, and one-off pieces, which he sells through galleries and exhibitions.

Turn a
Trunnion

DAVE REGESTER

An advanced exercise in spindle turning — the most difficult the author has undertaken . . .

Once you have mastered the turning of rings, you may ask yourself what you can ornament next in this way. You may not, but I did. I became obsessed with the idea of making rings within rings and the only way I could think of to achieve this was to make a box and turn a ring inside it. Those who are only concerned with making useful things need read no further.

The word trunnion is a technical term, not in common usage, denoting a projection on which anything can be pivoted. This is a mechanism found on big guns and, although applying the term to a box is hardly regular, it may be said to be a fairly accurate use. I only really adopted it because it sounds nice.

This is an example of spindle turning, albeit the most difficult I have ever done, so the same rules apply to selection of the timber as, for instance, in making a rattle. The wood, which needs to be hard, with a straight close grain, can be any one of a number of temperate hardwoods. The photos are of a piece of Yew 42mm $1\frac{5}{8}''$ x 42mm $1\frac{5}{8}''$ x 14mm $5\frac{1}{2}''$.

The blank needs to be mounted so that the top is free. In any case, the spindle through the middle will be too weak to support the sideways pressure of the tailstock. For this reason, the best way to mount the work is in a cup-chuck. This is a block of wood or metal with a morse taper hole through the middle. You can use the hole through the shaft of your lathe, if your bearings are strong enough, or make your own out of a piece of tough hardwood such as hornbeam as illustrated. This is held on a faceplate.

The blank needs to be roughed out between centres to fit the taper. I ensure I get a good fit each time by using a spanner as my sizing tool (photo 1). This has a bevel ground on one outside edge so that it will cut the wood to the correct diameter.

Photo 1
Cutting a Morse taper using a spanner as gauge

You support the spanner on the rest so that the unsharpened prong touches the work and then gently raise the handle so that the sharpened prong cuts into the wood. When the right diameter is reached, the tool stops cutting. **Provided you stand to one side you should be in no danger with this technique**. If you press too hard, the spanner will somersault across the workshop but then you will not be standing in its path, will you?

Photo 2
Cutting Morse taper using gauge

Photo 3
Inserting blank into chuck

The roughing gouge is used to cut the taper down to the reference diameter (photo 2) and the resultant blank is forced into the chuck (photo 3) with a hammer, rotating the blank while coshing to ensure a central placement. You then mount the chuck on the lathe and rough the blank to a cylinder, finishing fairly gently so that the surface is not too rough.

The Ring

The first feature to make is the ring on top of the box (see my previous article, page 51) and the shape of the top of the box (Photo 4, below).

Photo 4
The top of the box

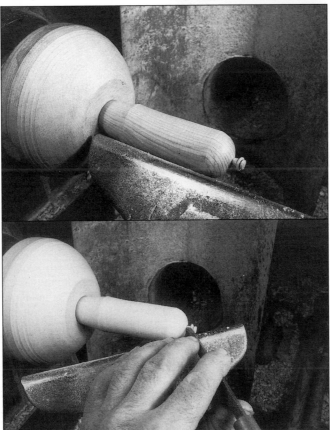

Photo 5
Starting the stem

The top of the box moves freely about the stem. This is achieved by cutting into the box top with the ring-making skew described in the previous article (see photo 5). You cut from the outside towards the centre at an angle of about 45°, with the point of the tool entering first.

Be sure to leave sufficient wood to form the stem. You do not have to go in to the full thickness of the top as you will be cutting from the inside to meet this cut later.

The Lid

You now need to hollow out the lid of the box, so you must establish the shape by cutting into the side at what will be the bottom edge (see photo 6). Use

Photo 6
Forming the lid

the skew with the point downwards as previously described and gradually widen a 'V' shaped cut. Bear in mind that the top must fit over the bottom and the cut at the bottom edge of the top should be at right angles to the axis or slightly overhung. This 'V' shape should be continued until it is wide enough to introduce the tool that will do most of the hollowing (photo 7).

Photo 7
Hollowing the lid

This tool is a straight chisel, ground on the bench grinder to form a cranked round nosed scraper (see drawing). It has a mirror-opposite partner which is used to hollow out the base. As you will see, it has a slight point that is used to cut into the lid along the stem and through to meet the cut started from the outside. There are no special rules about this tool. Just remember the basics of scraper usage, particularly that it should be used pointing down below the centre of the work. There is bound to be something of an overhang because the tool rest cannot be brought close to the point of contact. **So go steady!**

Square-ended Cranked Scraper

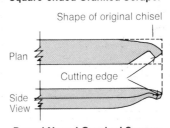

Round Nosed Cranked Scraper

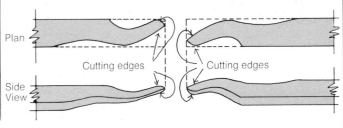

Photo 8
Cutting the lip

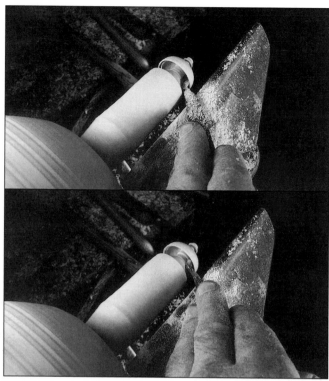

Photo 9
Cutting the stem inside the lid

Photo 10
The ring in the box

Photo 11
Hollowing the bottom

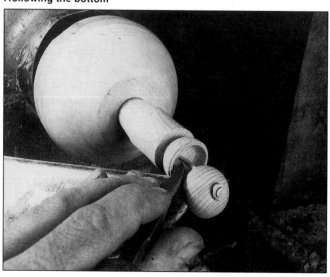

The Lip

After you have taken out some of the inside so that you can see the inside lip of the top, you must form the lip so that it fits over the base. This lip obviously has to be parallel to the axis of the lathe, so you need a tool with a right angle bend and a square end. Again this is ground from an old chisel (see illustration). The reason why you do this before you have taken much out of the inside of the lid is so that it is well supported while the cut is taking place (photo 8).

You can now continue with hollowing out the lid using the cranked scraper but **beware of removing the lip you have just formed**. It is very difficult to judge the thickness of the top since it is so small that you cannot get a pair of callipers in. I can only recommend that you go gently and use your eyes. The inside of the lid is formed using the right hand side of the scraper and the stem is formed using the point on the end (photo 9).

As you progress towards getting the correct thickness of the lid, ensure that your cuts are light ones and that the inside is as smooth as you can make it with the tool, as it is almost impossible to sand in there. When you eventually break through to the cut you made from the top it will be too late to correct any error.

The Stem

When the lid is free, you can make the stem using a modified skew. But leave a lump of wood near the bottom to make into the internal ring. You will find it useful to move the lid up and down the stem as it is formed to give you access to its length. The internal ring is now made in the usual way. When it is free you can continue the stem to ensure there is sufficient room in the lid to contain the ring and enable the lid to sit on the base so that you can form a lip on the base to accept the lip on the lid.

The Bottom

The heat generated in hollowing out the bottom will cause the wood to shrink slightly. So you must make the lid fit tightly before shaping the outside of the bottom to match the top. You can now move the rest right in close to the spindle between the lid and base (photo 11) and proceed to hollow out the bottom, using the cranked round-nosed scraper; the mirror image of the one used to hollow out the top.

As you can see from the photo of the trunnion boxes, you have much scope for exercising your imagination when it comes to the foot. I aim to make it look as though the stem passes through the bottom of the box and carries up to the top in a smooth line.

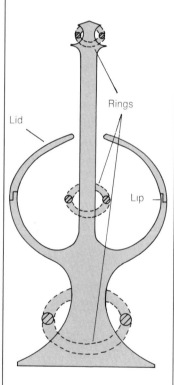

Rings

Lid

Lip

The only purpose of the trunnion box is to demonstrate your technical skill and design sense. If you are inspired to make one, perhaps you would care to send a photo to the magazine, and if the editor smiles upon your effort he might even be prepared to publish it. ∎

Repeat performance

Photo 1 *It's a challenge to make all the turnable parts for a large staircase such as this. The balusters are 75mm 3" wide.*

Photo 2 *A batch of 120 stair balusters requires discipline and perseverance, but it's a good way to practise turning skills.*

In the fourth and final part of his mini-series on spindle turning, Chris Pye describes how to turn items which are more truly 'spindly'.

So far I have looked at table legs, tool handles and bedposts to illustrate the ways in which a spindle turner tries to make the best use of his time.

I've dealt with spindles in the broad sense of the term, defining this in the first article as "anything spinning between centres". Now I come to items more truly 'spindly'.

These days, most staircases use balusters made on automatic lathes and most joiners, who are working to a price, will buy them, for they're usually much cheaper than hand-turned work. Indeed, I've seen finished stair spindles for sale at a price less than I can buy the wood for.

I confess to resenting customers who expect me to compete with the cheap (and sometimes, but by no means always, nasty) products of such lathes.

I find myself, quite reasonably, justifying my product and services: the different nature of the finished work, the possible variations in design and ease with which a hand turner can ring the changes, and the features that aren't possible on an automatic machine.

'I confess to resenting customers who expect me to compete with the cheap (and sometimes, but by no means always, nasty) products of such lathes'.

FIG 1 The tilted table of the bandsaw can be used to mark centres.

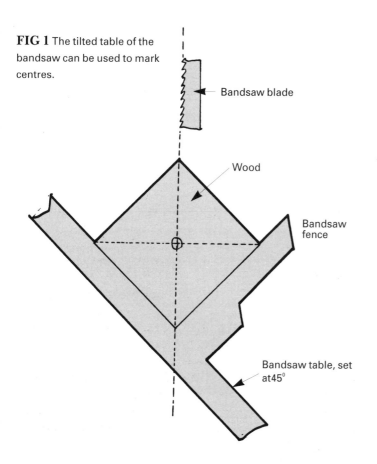

Bandsaw blade

Wood

Bandsaw fence

Bandsaw table, set at 45°

Photo 3 One of several sizes of centre-finding jig that can be easily made. The pin in the centre is a screw from beneath.

Photo 4 Centring a post in the jig.

Luckily there *are* discerning customers who appreciate the difference between hand and automatic work and will pay for it. And sometimes the price difference is not that great – especially on larger items, such as newel posts.

Stair balusters aren't always slender (Photo 1) and often the job involves different sizes of newel posts, with caps and drops, and possible diminishing lengths of baluster as the staircase approaches a ceiling.

So, all in all, turning the parts for a staircase can be a challenge, particularly when doing it to a price.

In this article I'll look chiefly at the balusters as slender turnings, which often give problems, and tell how I produce a run as fast as possible (Photo 2).

Not everyone is temperamentally suited to producing large numbers of repeat turnings – it puts many would-be spindle turners off. I'm borderline, enjoying this challenge of concentra-

tion and discipline now and then.

The way to overcome the threat of tedium is to concentrate harder and work faster, timing yourself and trying to beat the record. Repeat practice like this is the best way to improve skills.

The marking out of centres in repeat work can be time-consuming if you have scores, or hundreds, of pieces to do. A favourite method of mine is the self-centring punch, of which I have a range of sizes (Photos 3 and 4).

I usually leave it on the floor and dot

the blank in on the way from stack to lathe. The idea I took from Mike Darlow's excellent book *The Practice of Woodturning* (The Melaleuca Press 1985) which I'd recommend to all turners for the author's depth of understanding.

For smaller work such as stair spindles, the ends of which are cut to an angle anyway, I find my bandsaw is quicker (FIG 1).

Setting the table at 45 DEG, I adjust

▶

Photo 5 The drive centre pin protrudes enough to hang the spindle on without the prongs engaging.

Photo 6 I use a toolrest the whole length of the spindle, including the square pommels at either end.

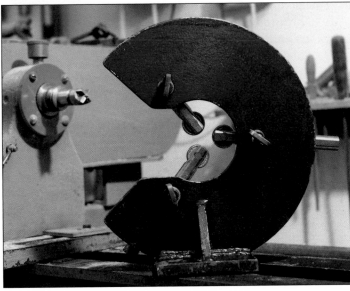

*Photo 7
A custom-made
steady. The
wheels in the
centre are
bearings, the
arms slide in and
out, pivot and
lock to get an
exact clamp of the
wood. A small
cylinder needs
to be created first
for the wheels to
run on.*

the fence so I can score the end of the wood from corner to corner, through the centre, with a gentle touch on the blade.

Turning the wood over onto the next corner I make a second slight groove through the centre, which is now marked. I then do the other end.

The time-honoured way is not to mark the centres at all but to make use of the extending centre pin in the drive centre. It's surprising how many turners overlook this important detail in drive centre design.

If you're not aware of it, look at the drive centre and you'll see the small pin in the middle extends beyond the radial prongs (Photo 5).

Besides lining up the centre to the wood, the extended prong allows it to be safely spun, even if the prongs are only lightly engaged.

This is useful for checking the wood's alignment because, until the prongs are driven home, the rotating wood can be easily and safely stopped with the hand or fingers reaching *under* the toolrest.

So begin with the pin, but barely the centres, engaged with the wood and start the lathe. The square wood should spin so the blur of the edges is as fine as possible.

If it appears the wood is not axially true, touch the offending end(s) with the point of the skew to mark the protruding corner – but don't mark a pommel.

Then stop the wood, tap the corner marked by the skew into its correct position, let the wood go, and tighten the tailstock.

I always check alignment in this way, even though I often mark the ends. If you can't stop the wood easily, the prongs are engaged too much. You'll need to ease back a little on the tailstock.

Large work

If the workpiece is large, heavy or long, you may have to stop the lathe to adjust the wood rather than risk hanging it on the drive centre pin.

For slender spindle turning, as elsewhere, I use a toolrest covering the whole length I'll be turning (Photo 6). This will usually include an amount of any square pommel.

One of the main problems with this sort of job is the whipping, caused by the wood's flexible nature. Indeed, in Photo 6, the workpiece (965mm 38" long by 32mm 1 ¼" across) can be bent at its centre some 20mm ¾" from the axis.

This deflection can bounce around the axis as the wood is spinning, creating a total deflection of twice this amount. The wood bends against the cutting edge rather than being cut, and tries to climb over the tool. Its elastic nature also causes the tail end to lag behind the drive end, adding to the problems.

Vibrating, whipping and chattering, unnerves many beginners and can put them off spindle work. Thicker, but longer sectioned, wood can be of the same proportions and be subject to the same problems. Such a piece can be more difficulty to control, as the forces are greater.

You can do several things to reduce this problem, such as keeping the speed of the lathe down, not having excess pressure from the tailstock and using light tool work. You can also support the wood and dampen vibrations.

When I started turning slender spindles I experimented with the old wooden wedge 'steady', the sort of thing seen in F.W. Pain's book, *The Practical Woodturner* (Evans Brothers Ltd, London 1957). I soon gave this up when I recalled that the best way to make fire and smoke was to rub two bits of wood together.

Later I made a steady (Photos 7 and 8) which I used when I couldn't support the wood enough with my hand. Many turners use this sort of device, and for beginners it can be helpful in getting a feel for working with vibrating wood, without the fear of the vibrations becoming uncontrollable or the wood breaking.

However, for a long time now, I have found a combination of using one hand to support the spindle, combined with sensitive toolwork with the other, eliminates vibration or reduces it to workable levels.

And it is with this in mind that I will describe my approach to turning slender spindles such as stair balusters.

I do nearly all my stair spindle turning with just two tools – a skew chisel

Photo 9 With these two tools I do most of my slender spindle turning.

and a small spindle gouge (Photo 9).

My skew is an old woodcarving tool, while the gouge is also old but has thicker walls than a carving tool. I suspect it was meant for pattern making.

You could use proper turning tools, but the important feature of mine is that they have short handles which sit snugly into one hand as I work.

Long handles

The normal long handles used by turners give control through leverage and are meant to be used with both hands. Here I want to use only one, the other hand supporting the wood, with the thumb guiding the tool.

I wrap my left hand lightly round the wood, letting it rest or travel along the toolrest to act as a sort of shock-absorber, dampening vibrations by linking the flexible wood with the solid metal toolrest.

My left thumb guides the skew or gouge in combination with my right hand (Photo 10). I usually extend my

Photo 10 Close up of how the skew chisel is held and manipulated.

right hand forefinger (or thumb, depending on the tool cut) along the blade.

I start the spindle by cutting the square pommels at each end, the one occasion when I hold the skew in the conventional way, with both hands.

Then, beginning on the left and still using the skew, I remove wood down to a cylinder so I can get a left-hand finger or two into a supporting position.

Up to this point the wood is at its thickest and I'm working near the ends – so there is little whipping or vibration.

I then start removing wood down to a cylinder with the skew, paring towards my left hand. I work towards the right of the spindle in sections of about a hand's width (Photo 11).

Each cut with the skew tapers from the original square section of the spindle down to a smooth cylinder. At the right hand end I reverse the skew to

▶

*Photo 8
The other side of
the steady*

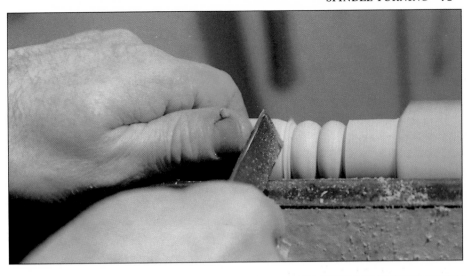

Photo 11 Paring off the square section to a cylinder with the skew chisel, working to the right in short sections. Note how my left hand is supporting both the wood and the tool while being supported in turn by the toolrest.

Photo 12 Cutting beads. The thumb is vital for control.

Photo 13 The spindle gouge is used in a similar way to the skew to cut coves.

finish up to the other pommel.

With this method I go from square pommel to smooth cylinder with the skew, without an intermediary roughing gouge.

For details on the baluster I use a prepared marking gauge, or marks on tape on the toolrest. Sometimes I use the skew width as a unit of measurement, as I have before.

I go straight on with the skew, holding it in a similar way to cut beads, fillets and slow curves (Photo 12). The left hand thumb is crucial to supporting and guiding the tool.

Skew

I go as far as I can with the skew, switching to the spindle gouge when it comes to cutting coves (Photo 13). The technique for the gouge is nearly the same. I rarely need more than these two tools.

You have to use all parts of your dampening hand on the wood so no one part of it overheats. It's not a matter of gripping the wood, which will cause friction and heat, but of calming

and coaxing it, rather like dealing with a fractious child.

While I work I have a sense of quite intimate contact and interplay between my hands, the wood and the tool. It's quite different from my experience when I'm turning conventionally, with both hands on the tool.

The close contact of my hands and the work smother the wood's vibrations and I have few problems with whipping. It's a technique which needs to be practised over and over.

When the spindle is finished, I return it to the lathe without stopping it, as I've described earlier, and off I go again.

For repeat turnings it's important to establish a rhythm, a flow of repeated, clean, precise actions that are refined as the work picks up speed.

Sometimes I notice I have switched to automatic pilot and can lose myself in the afternoon radio play, only to 'return' and find a pile of nicely turned spindles I don't remember doing. ∎

The author

Chris Pye has been both a professional woodturner and carver over some 16 years. He started with carving, owing his formative introduction to the master woodcarver Gino Masero, and a little later added woodturning.

He considers himself self taught, and equally at home in both crafts, often combining them.

Chris was born in Co. Durham but has lived a large part of his life in the South West of England. He has several years' experience teaching adult education classes in woodcarving, as well as private students in both turning and carving. In 1991 he demonstrated at the AWGB Seminar at Loughborough.

His first book, *Woodcarving Tools, Materials and Equipment* was published by GMC Publications last year.

Chris Pye,
The Poplars,
Ewyas Harold,
Hereford HR2 0HU.

Turn on th

HUGH FOSTER

Fed up with glass and plastic Christmas tree ornaments that get broken or crushed? Hugh Foster describes how to make the patterned wooden decorations turned by Bill Siehr.

Hugh Foster was born in Kansas and raised in suburban Chicago. He received a BA from Carthage College in 1966 and has been teaching English at Lincoln High School, Manitowoc, Wisconsin, ever since.
Hugh has been a woodworking hobbyist since 1967 and a woodworking author since 1984. He has had some 200 articles, reviews, project plans, tool manuals and books published since he took up the pen. Currently available worldwide is his *Biscuit Joiner Handbook*, published by Sterling in the US and Cassell in the UK. He has become increasingly interested in turning and is a regular contributor to *Woodturning*.

Readers will recall the articles on stickwork by Dick Bew in Issues 6 and 7 of *Woodturning*. When the glued up sticks or sections are sliced up, the result is end grain. The Christmas ornaments made by Bill Siehr also use pieces of different woods cut at interesting angles, but in this case it is the face grain that shows virtually everywhere on the ornaments' surfaces.

Bill started making the ornaments on a part-time basis at home. For about five years before his retirement he collected the offcuts that would otherwise have been burned at the boatyard where he worked as a cabinetmaker.

Now retired, Bill still runs his business, PolyWoods, from home making and selling up to 600 pieces a year at craft fairs and regional galleries. He has no intention of increasing pro-

duction so that making the ornaments is no longer fun.

Bill uses some exotic hardwoods in his work, but the pieces he uses are only ever offcuts or pieces with non-standard grain patterns that would otherwise have been burned, so there is no threat to the environment.

Supplies

When he needs to buy supplies he uses Woodcraft and Woodworker's Supply of New Mexico who supply small quantities for amateurs.

Bill does not have a workshop full of expensive specialist tools. He prefers to buy inexpensive tools and rebuild them to suit his purposes rather than try to buy precision. The result of this approach is that when things do go wrong he can usually repair or adapt the machine.

Bill loves to design projects at least as much as he loves to make them. He has lots of drawings made up, but he can't get to making them for want of time. I'm going to describe a couple of his Christmas ornaments in this article, and as I detail the making of them, you should be able to figure out how to make others.

Bill says the fun part of making almost any project is designing it and designing and making the required jigs and fixtures. He says seeing what you need is the requisite first step. Inventing the fixtures to an acceptable degree of accuracy is very engaging, but after that, some of the work can become rather tedious.

Using assembly line procedures, he makes from 25 to 50 pieces at a time, depending on how far the material he got out will go. But there are also lots of pieces in process — some have been glued up, ready to go for two years or longer, just waiting for either a need for the particular type of finished product or for time to machine them.

In Bill's shop there is only ½ to 1% waste because broken pieces are most often repairable. Bill has learned to repair nearly all the pieces that break on the lathe, because it's important to salvage pieces that already have the bulk of their work time in them.

How many varieties of ornaments will you be able to make after reading this article? That's hard to say, for the variety of his ornaments is hard to describe. He offers 50mm 2" and 75mm 3" versions of most of his models, and he makes them in such a variety of woods that you could have a dozen or more pieces of the same pattern ornament on the Christmas tree without having a duplicate.

'He makes them in such a variety of woods that you could have a dozen or more pieces of the same pattern ornament on the Christmas tree without having a duplicate.'

decorations

Here are the general shapes: teddy bears, flowers, and split plugs. Each of these is done with plugs — the split plug is made by cutting the wood to be cut into plugs with a jig saw, then gluing it back together with a piece (or several) of veneer glued into the saw kerf. He also makes a snowman with appropriately placed plugs of 25mm 1″ and 15mm ⅝″ and an acorn pattern.

Ornaments

There's an open bell pattern, and open ornaments that are turned, sawed, glued, and turned again. There are 50mm 2″ balls with variants on a dot theme, and 63mm 2½″ closed balls with stripes rather than plugs. Many of these hollow balls contain a metal air-rifle pellet so the ball will rattle when it is shaken.

Of course making projects like these involves more than just a lathe. His 12′ x 24′ basement workshop houses 11 stationary tools — all in *lots* of use. While a piece may involve only 10-12 minutes on the lathe, each piece takes at least one to two hours to make. Without a well-outfitted shop, it's sure to take even longer.

These turnings begin with accurately cut pieces of hex- or octo-stock. To cut these angles accurately, Bill uses a sliding table on his 200mm 8″ table saw. The first step in making almost any of these ornaments is cutting the small hex pieces. The requisite pieces for a 50mm 2″ ornament calls for us to rip a piece to about 48mm 1⅞″ wide, and to then cross cut it at 60 DEG into pieces 48mm 1⅞″ wide. With sanding, these pieces will finish to 45mm 1¾″.

Bill has built a jig for his 200mm 8″ table saw that cuts perfect pieces with each pass of

Photo 1 Bill Siehr using his circular saw table and mitre jig.

the saw (Photo 1). In this jig the piece to be cut sits on a pin to keep it from slipping. Additionally, the jig can be readily adjusted for hex or octagonal cutting.

Any saw marks or fuzz that would prevent tight gluing are sanded off, then the pieces are glued together and clamped with a hose clamp, or jubilee clip. Bill alternates wood species for interesting contrast effects (Photos 2 and 3).

After gluing up the main body the ends are sanded smooth on the belt sander (Photo 4) so caps can be added later, but ▶

Photo 4 The ends of the body are sanded ready for the caps.

Photo 2 Sections cut out ready to be glued into a hexagon.

Photo 3 The hexagon glued up and clamped with a hose clamp or jubilee clip.

Photo 5 A template is used for marking the positions of the holes which will be bored and then plugged.

before they are glued on the plugs which make up the design are put in.

First the design is marked on using a template (Photo 5). Bill's templates are of sheet metal which are cut to the exact size of the hexagonal pieces which make up the ornament's face.

The drilling and plugging is a tedious, time-consuming task. The holes are bored on the drill press, or pillar drill (Photo 6) then the plugs are inserted using an old bottle capper or corker (Photo 7). The plugs are made from many woods, but cedar is the prettiest for making flowers.

Photo 6 Holes are drilled and plugged in sequence.

Photo 7 An old bottle capper or corker is used to press in the plugs.

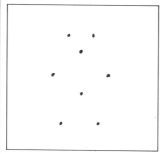

FIG 1 Pattern for making a template for the bear design.

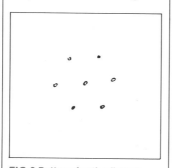

FIG 2 Pattern for the flower design. Drill and plug in the sequence given in the text.

Template patterns for making the bear and flower are shown in FIGS 1 and 2. For the bear, drill and plug in this order: 1) arms and ears 6mm ¼". 2) legs 8mm ⁵⁄₁₆". 3) head 12mm ½". 4) body 20mm ¾".

For the flower, drill and plug in 'this order: 1) first three alternate petals 12mm ½". 2) three remaining petals 12mm ½". 3) centre in contrasting wood 10mm ⅜".

In each case, after the first size listed has been drilled and the plugs glued in place they are bandsawn almost flush so the next stage of drilling and plugging can be done. When all the plugging is completed the hex sides are sanded flush and clean on the disc sander.

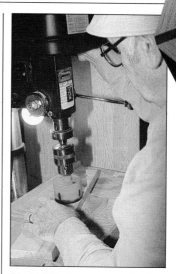

Photo 8 End caps are cut out with a hole saw. The wood should really be clamped down for safety when cutting.

Next the circular end caps are cut out on the drill press, or pillar drill, with a large hole saw from which the centre guide drill bit has been removed. Because he is familiar with the process, Bill has speeded up his operation by cutting these without clamps (Photo 8) but they really should be clamped or the wood can start spinning and cause injury.

The caps are glued on one at a time during the turning process which I will describe next. Getting the caps properly centred was a problem until Bill discovered Quick-Grip bar clamps (from American Tools who also make Vise-Grips). The beauty of these clamps is that there is no twist in their clamping action (Photo 9).

Photo 9 After the initial turning stages the caps are glued and clamped on.

Photo 10 End caps are turned concave on their insides before being glued on to the main body.

There are six chuckings involved in making each ornament. The first five are done in a 3 jaw chuck and the last between centres.

The first two chuckings are to turn the inside of both end caps concave (Photo 10). Then the first cap is glued on. Third, the body is chucked to true up the outside of the first cap. Fourth, the piece is turned 180 DEG and chucked by the first end cap so the inside of the body can be hollowed out and rounded.

Photo 11 The piece is mounted between centres for turning to a sphere.

Then the second end cap is glued on. Fifth, the piece is rechucked by the first end cap so that the centre of the second end cap can be found for the sixth and final work between centres (Photo 11). In total there is about 10mm ⅜" of waste stock at either end.

Bill spends only 10-12 minutes on turning each piece to a perfect sphere and measures each way with callipers only

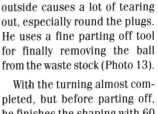
Photo 16 Some ornaments on the Christmas tree.

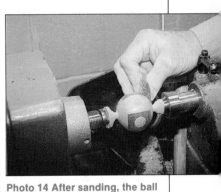

once (Photo 12). However, it is likely to take you or me a good deal longer! Although well practised, Bill says he has to develop a new eye with each turning session and each new size.

When asked about technique, Bill says simply, "Technique is what works for you." He turns using 'mainly small diameter gouges and a variety of parting tools on the outside of projects, and a round nosed scraper on the inside. Scraping on the

outside causes a lot of tearing out, especially round the plugs. He uses a fine parting off tool for finally removing the ball from the waste stock (Photo 13).

With the turning almost completed, but before parting off, he finishes the shaping with 60 grit abrasive, then works down through the grits to about 150 on most woods but to 220 on dense woods like cherry. Finally the piece is buffed with fine wire wool or ScotchBrite (Photo 14).

Photo 13 The parting off tool.

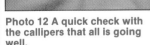
Photo 12 A quick check with the callipers that all is going well.

Photo 15 A display of Bill Siehr's ornaments and other turned items.

Photo 14 After sanding, the ball is buffed before parting off, oiling and waxing.

Bill prefers an oiled finish. He dips the balls in Danish oil, lets them sit for 30 minutes, then wipes them dry. The next day he repeats the process. After sitting for another day the balls are waxed, giving a finish that is easy to maintain.

The number of ornaments you will be able to make using this technique will depend on your desire, ingenuity, imagination and perseverance. If you keep at it you should be able to make enough to make lots of people very happy.

Bill Siehr, PolyWoods, 1923 South Fifteenth Street, Manitowoc, WI 54220, USA. ∎

THE MIN

DAVID DONNELLY

David Donnelly is a teleproductions manager at Boise State University, where he also teaches woodworking to adults in the Schools Community Education Program.

photos by David Donnelly

When small turnings require small tools, Steve Johnson is ready to provide either one.

Doll-house miniatures, almost microscopic in size, are the hallmark of Steve Johnson's turnings. Working in the shop behind his house in Meridian, Idaho, he shines a light into a miniature cocobolo goblet to show how the thin wood glows. 'This goblet is only 10-12 thousands of an inch in thickness', he explains. 'You can see how the light shines right through the wood.'

He's learned to use light and sound — not generally considered the primary tools of a woodworker — for achieving accuracy and aesthetic charm at such a small scale. 'As you turn the inside walls of a cup thinner and thinner,

the wood vibrates at a higher pitch.' And the thin walls are necessary to keep the miniatures in scale. By listening to the pitch, he can gauge the thickness and evenness of the sides of a goblet cup. Together, light and sound become a critical tool as he strives for uncanny accuracy and minute detail.

These are only a few of the unique tools that Johnson favours for miniature turning. As he described, 'When I started making miniatures, there was only one set of scrapers on the market. I bought them and didn't like them. So I started making my own out of concrete nails, then I upgraded to a broken tool bit. Finally I advanced to buying blank metal lathe boring bar tool bits.

Set of turning tools hand made by Steve Johnson

Depth gauge designed and made by Steve Johnson

Steve Johnson

Miniature ebony and cocobolo candlesticks and goblets, made by Steve Johnson. A US dime shows their scale ↗

Two kingwood needle cases, lilac sewing kit, and cocobolo crochet hook case ➡

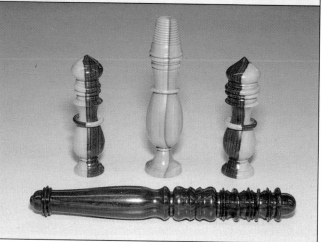

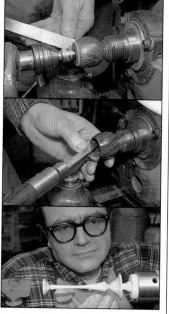

For his two-piece goblet, Johnson begins by turning the outside of the cup with a gouge and shear scraper

After turning the outside, Johnson turns the inside until the sides are a fine 10-12 thousands of an inch thick — thin enough to transmit light

Steve Johnson inspects the stem and base of his two-part goblet before separating it from the scrap

ATURE MAN

That's what I make my tools from today.'

With roughly six lathes in his shop, half of which are metal-working lathes, it's easy to see how his mind switches interchangeably between wood and metal faster than I could keep up.

HOME-MADE TOOLS

His home-made turning tools shine with the pride of creation, made all the more attractive with handles from a wide range of exotic woods. 'I built a grinder setup myself, so I grind my own tools from the blanks I buy. Then I hone and polish them. I used to make handles from all different kinds of exotic woods, but it's getting too hard to find them. So now I just use cocobolo. Even that's getting kind of scarce now. I also make my own ferrules from solid seamless brass tubing . . . So now I have a solid set of tools.'

As Steve demonstrated his turning techniques for the benefit of my camera, he chose to turn a two-piece cocobolo and maple goblet of a larger scale. The miniatures are nearly too small to see up close on a spinning lathe.

First, he turned the outside of the cocobolo cup and put a small tenon on the end. 'I used a gouge to turn the outside and got it as smooth as I could by using the side of the gouge as a skew. Then I used a shear scraper, which has a single-bevelled knife edge with no burr and is sharpened like a knife. I used it to level out the cut and make the final shape.' After finishing the outside, he sprayed it with lacquer and left it on the lathe to spin dry.

Inside, he hogged out the bulk of the wood with his scraper. 'I could have used a forstner bit attached to my tailstock, but by the time I got it set up I would have been half way finished with my scraper anyway.'

LISTENING

After hollowing it out, he resharpens the scraper with a burr. Starting at the outer lip of the cup, he turns inward to lay down the grain while listening to the pitch of the vibration. 'It's also important to start from the outer edge and cut inward because the thicker wood near the chuck adds support. If I thinned the inside first, the torque and strength of the wood would not tolerate heavy cutting towards the edge.'

The maple stem was turned with a small mortise in the end to support the tenon from the cup. The concave end of the stem matches the bottom of the cup precisely.

Intricate peach goblet required eight special hooked tools that Johnson made himself

Two-part cocobolo and maple goblet by Steve Johnson

Four-part lilac sewing kit (five if you count the ring)

TREASURE CHEST

Some of his favourite miniature pieces are shown in the pictures here, but even they cannot accurately capture the essence one feels by holding them, opening them up, and discovering a treasure chest of even smaller pieces inside. The sewing kit, for example, has a thimble cap on the top. Inside, there is a spindle for holding thread with another cap that hides an inner recess for needles. Tiny goblets and candlesticks of ebony, kingwood, and cocobolo, as well as larger two-part crochet hook cases and needle cases, have a consistent design theme that make them easy to recognise as his work.

Together, light and sound become a critical tool as he strives for uncanny accuracy and minute detail

'On miniatures, I may spend half a day working up a full-scale detailed drawing, and then put scaled dimensions on it.' One inch in real life becomes $\frac{1}{12}$in in doll house scale. 'I spend a lot of time searching for appropriate woods,' he said, 'I like lignum vitae, but oak doesn't work. In a small scale, the pores are too large. The better woods are ones with oil and close grain, such as rosewood, cocobolo, kingwood, and lilac.'

The large, full-size bowl with a concave top and narrow neck represents another style that Johnson favours, but does not find profitable because of the labour involved. 'I think this large bowl is peach. I wasn't really sure, so I took it out to my grandma's yard and tried to compare the bark on some trees she had out there.' In order to reach nearly inaccessible areas inside the bowl, he once again turned to his metal-working skill and made his own tools. 'This required bent tools, so I bent some cold-rolled steel to the shape I wanted. Then I set it up on the drill press, end bored it, and put a metal lathe bit in it. It works just fine.' He made about eight tools with different radiuses just for this bowl. 'After you've finally got the tools made, it still takes a long time to turn the bowl because you have to keep cleaning out the shavings.' But all is not lost since he plans to enter the bowl in a contest.

Making large and small tools to make large and small turnings. It's Steve Johnson's contribution to a brand of craftsmanship that is all too rare and unappreciated today. ■

Twist and rout

When Dutch woodturner Ger Vervoort was asked to barleytwist six long columns he didn't have a lathe big enough to do the job. Undaunted, he set about building extension bars and constructing a router-lathe.

GER VERVOORT

Ger Vervoort, 44, is an amateur woodturner living in Venlo, in the South of Holland. He works as a caretaker and maintenance man for a housing society and in his spare time does carpentry and furniture restoration.

Two years ago he built himself a lathe, but only found woodturning fun after he had met a woodturner demonstrating at a craft fair who showed him some good turning tools (Henry Taylor) and showed him how to use them.

From him, Ger bought some tools and a book called *Woodturning in Pictures,* by Bruce Boulter. Reading this and experimenting with the tools got him hooked on woodturning.

Now he has several books and a complete set of Dennis White videos.

Unfortunately, Ger cannot spend the time on woodturning he would like to, but whenever he can he loves to get behind the lathe.

Ger proudly displays the six columns.

It was an order which called on all my experience. To turn and barleytwist six oak columns (about 1,500mm 59" long x 80mm 3 ⅛" DIA) as part of the decoration for a pub's huge wall cabinet.

I had to overcome several problems to make them, not the least being my lathe which could turn pieces only 950mm 37 ⅜" long. And with this length of column I'd need a steady centre — which I didn't have.

Because twist making is mainly handwork and very time consuming, I had to come up with a construction with which I could, for the greater part at least, rout them. I also had to complete the order in the few days before my holiday.

Up to then, my experience of making twists was practically zero, consisting of making one copy of a chairleg. A great help to me, was Dennis White's demonstration video (No 6) on twists, and Chris Pye's *Carving on Turning* article on barley twists in Issue 19 of *Woodturning.*

My next problem to overcome was the capacity of my lathe. I extended the bed bars to create a distance between centres of at least 1,500mm 59".

As it was for a short time only, I kept the extension simple, using small wooden beams of the same dimension as the bed bars, which are 70mm 2 ¾" x 40mm 1 ⅝". With another two small beams I clamped it all together with bolts and F-clamps.

The end of the extension bars were supported with a piece of 40mm 1 ⅝" thick plywood of the right length. With this construction it wasn't possible to slide the toolrest over the full length of the column, so I had to reverse them after turning halfway (Photo 1).

LIGHT CUTS

When I accepted the order, I presumed I'd need a steady centre, but because I didn't have one, I had to make one. I first tried to turn without it and found this was possible when I made light cuts in the mid section of the column. These little unevennesses would disappear when the twists were cut.

Turning was done with the roughing gouge only, and then coarse sanded with a 125mm 5" sanding pad in a drill. While turning, it was necessary to support the tailstock with some beams

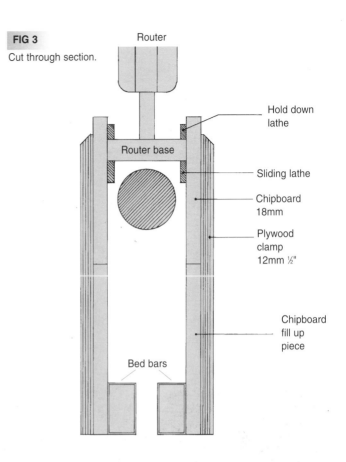

FIG 3
Cut through section.

Router

Hold down lathe

Router base

Sliding lathe

Chipboard 18mm

Plywood clamp 12mm ½"

Chipboard fill up piece

Bed bars

Photo 1 The lathe extension and the column before I started turning. You can see why I had to reverse the column after turning halfway.

FIG 1
My lathe with the extension.

Workpiece

Handwheel

Wooden cylinder

250mm 9 ¾"

1500mm 59"

850mm 33 ⅜"

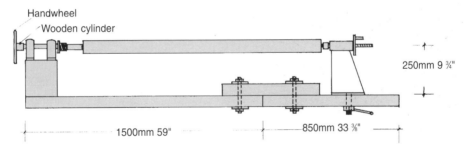

FIG 2
The router carriage from the top and front.

2200mm

Wire

Router

Wind around cylinder

200mm 8"

230mm 9"

Wheels, about 40mm 1 ⅝" DIA

Wire

Clamp

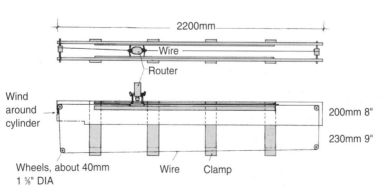

between the walls of my workshop, to prevent shaking (Photo 2).

Turning was the easiest part. Now I had to build a large router-lathe. I first looked at pictures of them and decided

the construction would not be too intricate.

After some sketching and calculations (see FIGS 1 - 3) I came up with a simple construction which could easily be built on to my lathe. Just like

▶

Photo 2 I braced the tailstock with some beams to hold it steady.

the extension bars, this was to be used only once, so I made my router carriage from cheap chipboard.

The router could slide along this carriage the full length of the workpiece. The router was moved by a 2mm steel wire, connected on one side of it and guided over wheels beneath the lathe and back to the other side of the router (Photo 3).

Simultaneously with the router movement, the workpiece had to rotate. To achieve this combination of movements I replaced the driving pulley by a cylinder on which the steel wire was wound around.

So, standing at the front of the lathe, the router slid above the column, and the steel wire was connected on the right side of the router base.

From here, the wire was guided to a wheel at the right end of the carriage, down over the second wheel underneath the extension bars, to the third wheel at the left side under the lathe.

This third wheel was placed under the cylinder at the driving end. The wire went up, wound around the cylinder, was guided over the fourth wheel, came right above the cylinder to the left side of the carriage, and back to the left side of the router base.

The steel was tightened up with a wire tightener. Next to the cylinder I placed a hand-wheel, which rotated the column and simultaneously moved the router.

The diameter of the cylinder

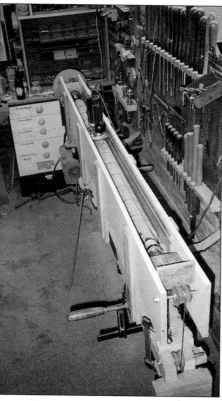

Photo 3
The router carriage, routing the straight groove. You can see the steel wire and the wheels over which it was guided.

Photo 4
A closer look, after I'd routed the V-groove.

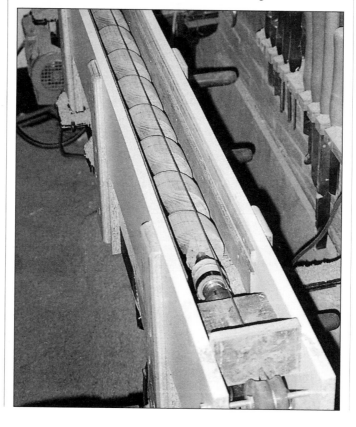

around which the wire was wound determined the distance of router movement in relation to the rotation of the column. The outer ridge which winds around the twist is called the bine, and the distance between two bines in a straight line is called the pitch. I decided to make the distance of the pitch 1½ times the diameter of the column.

To define the diameter of the cylinder I made the following calculation: diameter of column 80mm 3⅛", the pitch is 1½ x 80mm 3⅛" = 120mm 4¾". This means the circumference of the cylinder also has to be 120mm 4¾". As I knew the circumference, I reversed the normal formula (which is 3.14 x DIA = circumference) to find the diameter of 38.2mm (i.e. circumference ÷ 3.14 = 38.2 mm DIA).

Routing was done in several stages with different bits. As I have a light-duty 900 watt router with a 8mm collet, I couldn't use heavy cutters which match the pattern.

So I started with an 8mm straight bit to rout a groove of the right depth. Next, with a 45 DEG bit, I took away the sides of this groove, so I had a big V-groove with a flat bottom (Photo 4).

Hollowing the bottom of the groove and rounding the top edges was done with a cove bit (Photo 5). It wasn't really a practical tool for the top edges, but I didn't have any alternative.

Making light cuts, I got as close as I could to the desired pattern. For each cut after that I had to readjust the router,

'Because twist making is mainly handwork and very time-consuming, I had to come up with a construction with which I could, for the greater part at least, rout them.'

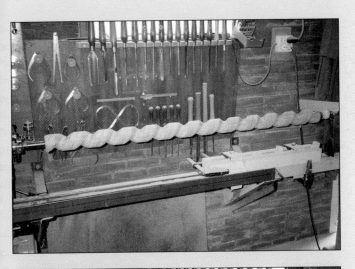

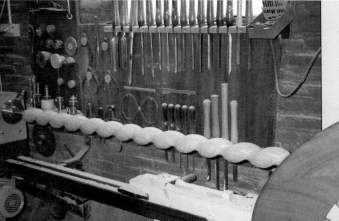

**Photo 5
With routing fin-
ished, I started
rasping and
sanding.**

**Photo 6
The completed
column.**

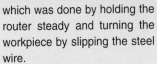

which was done by holding the router steady and turning the workpiece by slipping the steel wire.

Now I faced the physically hardest part of the job — rasp-ing and sanding the twists. The coarse part was done with the lathe stationary, and the finer — using grits up to 220 — with the lathe running at low speed (Photo 5 and 6).

The whole operation took about 40 hours. I worked 4 ½ days on it, then closed my workshop and took my well-deserved holiday.●

A selection of Ger Vervoort's work.

After his childhood in Derbyshire and Nottinghamshire, Geoff Yeomans went to sea to see the world at the age of 16 and served in the Merchant Navy for six years, including war service as a 3rd Mate.

After the war he trained and worked in horticulture for six years doing mainly decorative work. He moved from the Midlands to work at Wye College and Wisley until a motorbike crash cut short his career.

He then went to teacher training college and taught rural science in secondary schools for nearly 30 years before taking early retirement nine years ago. Geoff and his wife have lived in their Kent farmhouse cottage for 34 years.

His trading name, Albion Woodturning, comes from the old name for England, and a ship, the Albion Star, in which he once sailed.

This mini lathe runs at 2100 RPM off a car electric aerial motor and battery. It is ideal to teach youngsters to turn on.

TURNING BACK THE CLOCK

NICK HOUGH

Geoff Yeomans has no mains electricity, gas or water at his 17th Century home, but he still enjoys 20th Century power woodturning in his workshop. Here's how he does it.

Lace bobbins are a speciality.

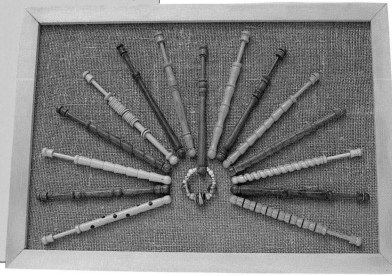

For most of us, selection of a lathe revolves around such things as capacity, power, heaviness and rigidity, speeds and so on. But Geoff Yeomans has a different criterion. He has no mains electricity in his home or workshop.

Come to that he has no mains gas or water either at his 300-year-old farm cottage buried deep in the Kent countryside, so many of the other things we take for granted at the flick of a switch also require some thought for Geoff and his wife.

Necessity is the mother of invention, and ingenuity is the name of the game in Geoff's workshop. All his equipment that cannot be hand or foot powered is run by petrol engines or batteries.

Geoff's pole lathe in the garden.

"If you haven't got something you want and you can't get it or afford it, you jolly well have to make it. And if you can't make it then you will have to find something else to do."

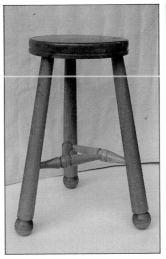

This ususual English elm stool is one of the largest items made by Geoff. It is 460mm 18" high x 255mm 10" DIA.

These 1/12 scale miniatures won the bronze medal at the Woodworker show last year.

Geoff's workshop showing the lathes and belt drive system from the petrol engine.

He has three Arundel woodturning lathes and has just acquired a Drummond metal turning lathe. The largest, 30" Arundel can turn at speeds from 500 to 2,000 RPM and the middle one has speeds ranging from 800-3,500 RPM.

Both are powered by a 4-stroke, 78cc Suffolk motor mower engine which produces over 1 hp at 3,000 RPM, but Geoff says he doesn't need to run it at more than 1,800 RPM. He can get his middle lathe running at 2,000 RPM with the motor little more than ticking over because it does not need anything like the power required for mowing grass.

This middle lathe has five steps on the headstock pulley and two on the countershaft pulley, giving 10 combinations. More power can be obtained at the same speed by dropping a step and opening the throttle a little. This lathe can take 355mm 14" between centres and 178mm 7" over the bed and is used more than the other two.

Car battery

The smallest Arundel, which Geoff uses for turning miniatures and lace bobbins, has a single speed of 3,000 RPM and runs off a 12V motor from a lorry windscreen wiper. It can run on a car battery for eight hours before recharging. Geoff's eldest grandson has been using this lathe since he was just five.

Geoff has clocks and gauges which tell him how long he has turned and when he will need to fill up with fuel or recharge. This also keeps a handy record of the time he spends turning, and it works out at around 400 hours a year, or eight hours a week on the lathe.

The mower motor runs over six hours on a quart of petrol, and this works out at about 10-15p per hour for fuel, including oil, depending on the size of work being turned.

Tool sharpening? Geoff simply hooks up his grinder to the lathe with a drive belt and pulleys.

Geoff first saw a petrol engine being used by a ropemaker and so was familiar with the idea. When he took up turning and had no electricity it seemed the natural thing to do.

"If you haven't got something you want and you can't get it or can't afford it, you jolly well have to make it. And if you can't make it then you will have to find something else to do", is his philosophical comment.

Wouldn't change

"A friend of mine in the village has a Record No 1 lathe which he lets me use from time to time. I must admit it's easier to use, but I've got used to my own system now and I wouldn't want to change."

Geoff went to school with Douglas Arundel, who founded the famous lathe firm just after the war. They both got interested in turning after watching the woodturner at their local woodyard. Geoff made his first treadle lathe from an old bicycle when still a teenager — obviously an innovator even then.

His largest lathe is 44 years old and one of the first 100 produced by Douglas Arundel. His other two are just three years old.

Despite his lifelong interest in turning, Geoff did not pursue the craft for some 30 years while bringing up two sons and a daughter, except for a few toys for his children. But he plunged back into the work seriously after taking early retirement nine years ago and now makes toys and dolls house furniture for his grandchildren.

While his interest is part-time and amateur, he refuses to call it a hobby. "Hobbies are things people do for a change when they come home from work and to take their mind off the day", he says.

"For me this is therapy. It keeps me active and gives me a sense of achievement without a lengthy process. I can make something useful quite quickly and at the end of the day I can say I have done something and not wasted my time." ▶

"I don't go out with the idea of selling to make a big profit. Most of my demonstrations are for charity."

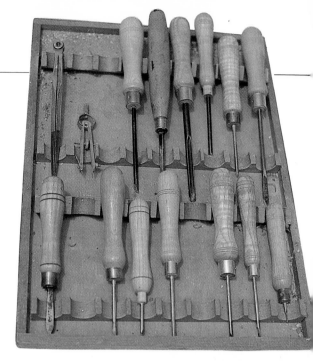

Geoff has been a model maker all his life and now specialises in smaller turned items like pen and flower holders, lace bobbins, boxes, light pulls and so on, and also miniatures. A set of his $\frac{1}{12}$ scale dolls house furniture won the bronze medal at the national Woodworker show last year.

He does demonstrations for local church and school fêtes under the name of Albion Woodturning and has done the odd demo for The Turning Point and the Kent branch of the AWGB, but he does not do craft fairs.

"I don't go out with the idea of selling to make a big profit", he says. "Most of my demonstrations are for charity and I sell just enough to cover my costs of tools, materials and running the workshop. I get the odd private commission for stools or handles or candlesticks and suchlike, and I aim to just about break even over the year."

The largest work he can turn is 255mm 10" DIA, and 760mm 30" long. His largest items are stools, stair spindles and bowls. But of course there is no power sanding in this workshop!

Built workshops

Over the last 30 years Geoff has built his own garage and workshops, 90% of which came from recycled materials. He also makes most of his own tools for miniatures from masonry nails and home-turned handles.

Geoff and his wife's home was built around 1700, and was once a farmhouse with its own dairy and a thatched roof. The cooker and fridge are powered by bottled gas, and another petrol engine pumps water from their own well.

They have a solid fuel boiler for heat and hot water, and they keep a 40-gallon store of paraffin for their lamps which light home and workshop.

Some of Geoff's miniature turning tools, most of which are home made.

But of course there is no washing machine, vacuum cleaner or electric iron!

In the workshop lamps hang from hooks at strategic places in the ceiling. An old cymbal bought at a jumble sale stops the heat from setting the roof on fire, and an old adjustable car mirror reflects light on to the workpiece. However, Geoff prefers to work by daylight and only does roughing out work by lamplight.

Home and workshop are surrounded by an aura of peace and quiet, broken only by the barking and grunting of foxes and badgers at night, and the steady chugging of a lawnmower engine ticking over by day . . . ■

A selection of Geoff's turned items in ripple ash, wild cherry, oak, pine, banksia nut, field maple and cupressus lawsoniana.

The petrol engine fits neatly under the bench containing the two larger lathes — the exhaust goes outside, of course. The battery-run lathe is on the left.

Geoff made this working model of a woodturner, powered by four torch batteries. "People say he looks like me", he says.

- + ALBION WOODTURNING + -

GEOFF HEATH

**Involuted, or inside out turning, is an unusual technique,
the do's and don'ts of which Geoff Heath describes here.**

INSIDE OUT

Very few examples of 'inside-out' or 'involuted' turning have been published in *Woodturning*, apart from Tobias Kaye's definitive article, *Within Every Acorn an Oak Tree* (Issue 11). It's an unusual technique I recommend your readers to try.

Inside-out turning is where you take a length of square section, turn it between centres, split it lengthwise into four smaller squares and glue these together again so that what were the outer four edges now meet in the middle.

Holes appear in the outer surface through which the inside can be seen. The reconstituted square is then turned into a new shape.

Readers who try it may find the following points useful.

1. Split the square block into four smaller squares first of all, and glue these together in the 'inside-out' configuration before turning. After the first turning, the squares are re-assembled in their original positions for the second turning.

The advantage of this approach is that the finished article has a matching grain pattern throughout the piece. ▶

Photo 7 Batch of finished Christmas tree decorations.

Saw-cuts will interrupt this pattern slightly, but the interruption will be less obvious if straight-grained timber is used. If the timber is also quarter-sawn, so much the better.

Before starting to turn, plane the re-assembled block on all four faces to make it truly square. This will ensure the best possible fit of the joints in the final assembly. It will also reduce the chances of a good grain match, so don't overdo it. Take care to remove an equal amount from each face so the block remains centred on the glue-lines.

2. Before tackling an 'inside-out' project, you need to know what its final appearance will be, especially the shape of the pierced 'windows'.

You can gauge the shape of these by looking at the space created by turning. To see this space, place a straight-edge along the upper surface on the turned block (Photo 1).

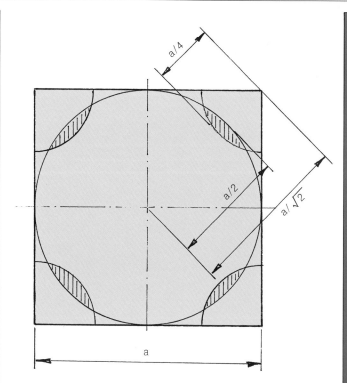

FIG 1 Section through a block showing the four ligaments after a 50% reduction in diameter during the first turning.

Photo 1 A block after the first turning. A straight edge reveals the negative of the half-window profile.

If you see a semi-circular cove, this will make a circular window, while a V-notch will make a diamond-shaped one, and a square channel a rectangle.

All other windows are combinations of these basic shapes. Wherever a 'flat' remains after the first turning, there will be no window.

3. It's important the corners of the square section are untouched at the ends of the workpiece during the first turning, for when the four pieces are re-assembled, these corners meet along the centre-line.

If the corners were turned away, the ends of the reconstituted block would have cusped holes at their centres, making it difficult to support the workpiece. So leave the ends square the first time round.

4. When the pieces are re-assembled for the second turning, the workpiece contains four ligaments which join the two ends together, the windows (i.e. the spaces between these ligaments) being centred on the glued joints.

FIG 1 shows a section through the ligaments at a point where the first turning has reduced the local diameter of the workpiece to 50% of the thickness of the square block.

A little arithmetic reveals that the thickness of the ligament is then no more than 0.043 times the width of the block, assuming the outside diameter of the finished article is the maximum which can be obtained from the original square.

Thus a 50mm 2″ square block would have a ligament only 0.086″ thick, and any shaping of the outside of the workpiece would reduce this (and the width of the ligament) still further, leading to another potential masterpiece being consigned to the scrap-bin.

Fortunately, quite small changes in the minimum diameter created by the first

Geoff Heath is a self-taught turner who has been improving his skills since he took up the craft as a hobby in 1975.

He began woodturning as a relaxation from his job as Chief Structural Engineer at the Woodford factory of British Aerospace, and since he retired in 1988 he has been able to spend more time at his hobby.

However, it still has to compete with his other interests of choral singing, attending an art class, committee work for his local residents' association, and domestic chores including gardening.

Geoff has always been interested in ingenious ways of doing things, which is probably why he has found such satisfaction in inside-out turning. He believes he must have an involuted mind, as this style of turning comes naturally to him.

It also explains the nom-de-plume he uses elsewhere in *Woodturning* — crossword compilers need to think in a skewed fashion, he says.

Geoff is a founder-member of the High Peak Woodturners. He is also a Chartered Engineer, a Fellow of the Institution of Mechanical Engineers, and a Fellow of the Royal Aeronautical Society.

turning make substantial differences to the thickness of the ligaments. If the minimum diameter is increased from 50% to 60% of the thickness of the block, the ligament thickness is more than doubled.

A further increase to 75% raises the ligament thickness to 0.168 times the thickness of the block — almost four times the 50% value.

However, these larger diameters may produce windows which are too small to be of any significance. So remember, for the diameter of the first turning, 50% is too much and 75% is not enough.

If that sounds nonsensical, just remember we are thinking inside-out!

5. Accurate alignment of the two halves of each window must be achieved on re-assembly, or the 'stepped' appearance of the windows will ruin the finished job. Windows are not staircases, so don't put steps in them.

Preparation

To saw the basic block into four squares, you need to set the fence of the bandsaw at half the width of the block. I cut a thin (3mm ⅛″) slice off the end of the block, lay it flat on the table, guess the setting of the fence, and saw a trial notch in one edge.

I then turn the piece over, and repeat the process. If the two notches don't coincide, the fence can easily be adjusted until they do.

Even if I don't get it right the first time, I've still got three more edges left. Once the fence is set, the four squares can be cut, and I label them A, B, C and D on their inner corners as shown in Photo 2.

Despite what I said about not touching the corners near the ends of the workpiece, I must admit to a small departure from point 3: I cut a tiny chamfer on the outer corners of both ends of all four squares. When the

Photo 2 Basic block after cutting into four square sections. Inner corners are labelled.

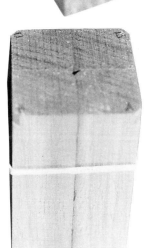

Photo 3 Block re-assembled for the first turning. Labels are now on the outer corners.

squares are assembled into the 'inside-out' block there is thus a small square hole at each end, bang in the middle (Photo 3).

This ensures the driving and tail centres locate accurately. It's best if the driven end has a larger hole than the tail end.

I then carry out one further operation on each small square: I cut a diagonal line across the unlabelled end. This provides a location for one blade of a four-pronged driving centre.

The squares can now be

glued together, care being taken to assemble them in the correct orientation. I put them together the original way round first of all (guided by the letters A, B, C, D) and then rotate each separate piece through 180 DEG until the letters appear in the outer corners.

A further check is that the diagonal cuts should form a cross on the driven end (Photo 4).

I have tried two methods of assembly — the well-esta-

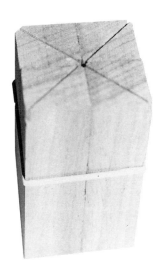

Photo 4 Driving end of the re-assembled block showing diagonal cross.

blished one of paper glued between the squares, and glue on its own. The first method has the advantage of enabling the squares to be split apart very easily after the first turning.

There is no need to scrape off the remains of the paper, since it appears on the external faces of the reconstituted block, from where it is removed during the second turning.

> 'Accurate alignment of the two halves of each window must be achieved on re-assembly, or the "stepped" appearance of the windows will ruin the finished job.'

However, I soon realised that the block can be sawn apart along the glue-lines without harming the finished job, thus dispensing with the need for a paper interlayer. I use Hot Stuff Special T (gap-filling) with Hot Shot accelerator in the interest of speed.

I first glue A to B, and then C to D. It's essential to get their internal faces in the same plane. A flat surface is needed here, pressing the two squares down on it and then sliding them towards each other until they touch.

Suitable surfaces are offered by the tables of the bench drill or the bandsaw, but if you're using superglue, be careful not to stick the workpiece to the table.

The two half-blocks AB and CD can then be glued together, after which the re-assembled block should be planed on all faces in keeping with point 1, although I must confess that for the small items depicted in the photographs, I got away without any planing. As a final touch, the outer corners should be chamfered as before.

First turning

Now it's time to put the workpiece in the lathe. The four-pronged driving centre ▶

acting on the diagonal cross will not cause any splitting action, since its point is too small to touch the sides of the central square hole.

The tail centre is the problem, since its wedge action could easily split the piece open along the glue-lines if the tailstock were to be over-tightened.

I therefore use a ring centre, which helps to hold the four squares together. I prefer the hollow kind which comes in a long hole boring kit, since it has a retractable centre point.

I use this point to locate the square hole in the end of the workpiece, and then allow the centre to retract as I wind the tailstock forward to engage the ring centre. A little grease on the ring minimises friction.

At last we can start the lathe — and about time, too, you're probably thinking. The first step is to turn the central area down to a near-circular section which has narrow 'flats' in the region of the glue lines.

In point 3 I warned you to confine your action to this central area, and to leave the ends alone. With the required window shape in mind, its negative shape can now be turned (point 2), remembering the limits on the minimum diameter (point 4).

When the first turning is complete, there are two options: to finish the surface in the normal way with sealer and polish, or to paint it.

Normally, I'm opposed to painting my turned articles, believing the wood should speak for itself, but if the interior is rather dark, some highlighting could be useful.

Reconstitution

After the first turning, the block is split into four again on the bandsaw, and re-assembled in the original orientation (Photo 5) with point 5 in mind. The glue must be spread evenly over the whole of the

Photo 5 Reconstituted block showing the windows.

mating areas, otherwise some 'dry' joints may appear in the finished article.

Alignment is made easier if the ends of each half-window are cut at right-angles to the surface during the first turning.

Shallow sloping cuts will not meet exactly if the first block was not centred properly, or if the original four squares were not quite the same size.

Close inspection of Photo 5 reveals that what appears to be a star-shaped window with pointed ends actually has small flats at the end of each arm.

Second turning

The block is returned to the lathe, and the outer surface turned, a mental note being kept of the extent of the internal space so the ends are not cut too thin.

My chief concern is that the bevel of my chisel tends to drop into each window as it passes, causing the cutting edge to dip slightly.

This means I cut deeper into the ligaments than I intend, creating an unwanted hollow. My solution to this problem is to hold the chisel firmly at the required angle, allowing it to 'float' across the window region

without support from its bevel.

Up to now, I haven't told you what I was making when I took the photographs. This was my first serious attempt at 'inside-out' work, and I was trying my hand at a few Christmas tree decorations.

These were roughly the shape and size of an egg, turned from nominally 50mm 2″ square stock cut into blocks 90mm 3½″ long. I used three different exotic woods: padauk, sonokeling rosewood, and zebrano.

To try the effect of painting the interior, I coloured the padauk gold, the rosewood silver, and the zebrano red, using the enamel sold for model aircraft kits (Photo 6).

Photo 6 Indian rosewood block after initial turning, with turned surfaces painted silver.

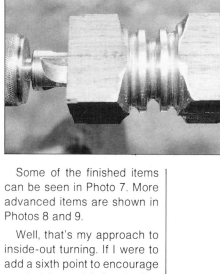

Some of the finished items can be seen in Photo 7. More advanced items are shown in Photos 8 and 9.

Well, that's my approach to inside-out turning. If I were to add a sixth point to encourage you to take up this fascinating process, it would be:

Don't be an outsider – turn the inside first! ∎

Photo 8 Inside out candlestick in cocobolo.

Photo 9 A pair of inside out table lamps.

Weed pot wonders

Decaying logs and branches need not be rejected for turning. They can be used to make hollow weed pots, as Kai Kothe describes.

Half-rotten branches and logs from diseased trees can be turned into hollow weed pots in which to display dried flowers or grasses (Photo 1). And you don't need to use special deep hollowing tools.

First, select a fairly round, weathered branch that has lost its bark. Hollow logs with the bark still on can be used, but check that it's firmly attached.

Logs about 100-150mm 4"-6" DIA are ideal, provided the thickness left by the rot is about even. Don't worry about the small splits you always find in decaying wood, as they shouldn't decrease stability.

Branches with big splits running along their length should be rejected, however, as the wood might disintegrate on the lathe.

Preparation

Cut a suitable length with a bandsaw or chainsaw, and then decide where the top and bottom of the weed pot should be, turning it in your hand to envisage its final shape.

As well as aesthetic considerations, you also need at this stage to consider practicalities. Try to choose the thickest part for the bottom because it will need to be held in a chuck later on.

I use a two-prong drive made by Craft Supplies for their precision combination chuck. It has an extra centre point that is longer than the two prongs and can be adjusted or

▶

Photo 1 A selection of the author's weed pots.

Photo 2 Fix your toolrest at right angles to the lathe bed.

Photo 3 Now move the toolrest parallel to the lathe.

Photo 4 Drill shallow holes into the wood to enable the prongs to grip it tightly.

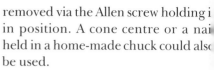

removed via the Allen screw holding it in position. A cone centre or a nail held in a home-made chuck could also be used.

Place your blank between centres and fix the toolrest at right angles to the lathe bed (Photo 2). Now turn the blank while watching its distance from the toolrest.

Move the blank between the centres until you get a roughly equal distance over the whole 360DEG turn. By following these steps you determine the plane in which the foot will be.

Now move the toolrest to a position parallel to the lathe's axis (Photo 3) and turn the blank again to check whether it is centred. This might not be important on a heavy lathe that can be operated at low speed, but much more overhang on one side than the other will cause heavy vibrations on a light lathe.

Saw off any unwanted wood when you remove the blank from the lathe if it isn't centred.

Now loosen the centre point's holding screw on the two-prong drive and turn the tailstock handwheel until the prongs leave their marks on the wood.

Remove the workpiece from the lathe and use these marks to drill shallow holes into the wood so the prongs really grip it (Photo 4). With this project, you don't want to apply too much

Photo 5 A flange has been turned to hold the workpiece.

Photo 6 The tail centre is used for added support and safety.

Photo 7 After the corners have been rounded, you can increase the speed.

Photo 8 Keep your fingers out of the danger area.

pressure from the tailstock because this will deform or even break the blank.

Photo 5 shows the blank remounted and a flange that has been turned at the tailstock end to hold the workpiece.

Always start the lathe at a low speed (about 400-700RPM) and be prepared to stop it immediately if there is heavy vibration – or worse.

If you use a blank with bark on it, try to leave almost the full thickness of the bark at the bottom, as this gives the finished pot a more balanced appearance than a thin strip. You can achieve this by turning a recess until you reach solid wood and placing the flange inside it.

I prefer to use the chuck in a contracting mode, because this doesn't enlarge splits that might already be in the wood. It's easier, of course, if there are no cracks, to use expanding jaws.

But you have to be very careful, because the remaining cone, held by the tail centre, consists of half bark and half rotten wood that breaks easily when a tool catches.

This happened once to me. The

workpiece flew off the lathe, shot out of the workshop through the open door and split apart when it struck the concrete garden path. Luckily, it didn't cause any damage.

Now you need to turn the workpiece around and hold it in a chuck. The Mick O'Donnell jaws available as an accessory for the APTC Super Precision Chuck work fine, allowing access right to the bottom of the workpiece. Use the tail centre for added support and safety (Photo 6).

Turning and sanding

You can use nearly all the usual bowl turning techniques – even shear scraping with a wide scraper, but your cuts should be light.

After rounding the corners and balancing the workpiece at low speed, you can increase speed to about 1,000 - 2,000RPM, depending on the condition and size of your workpiece (Photo 7).

Once you have reached the final dimensions, except at the top, where the tailstock support is still needed, you can start sanding. It's safest to do this by hand with the lathe at rest.

A more adventurous approach is to run the lathe at about 1,000RPM and sand with various grits wrapped round a big cork sanding block. Avoid catching the block's corners or the sandpaper in the workpiece by bringing only the middle of the block in contact with it.

Start sanding at the more solid areas around the bottom and the top, and move the sandpaper carefully towards the hollow areas as far as your nerves can stand. Ensure your fingers are kept out of the danger area (Photo 8).

▶

The author

Kai Kothe, of Kelkheim, Germany, teaches electrical engineering and English in vocational training. His interests in technology and English took him, in 1980, to the Centre for Alternative Technology, in Machynlleth, Powys, Wales, where he has since returned several times as a volunteer worker.
The centre had a small woodturning lathe on which Kai 'played around' after work, during his first visit. He soon became hooked on woodturning.
Back in Germany, he bought a lightweight second-hand lathe which handled turning between centres quite well.
The availability of green wood after severe storms led to him experimenting with this kind of turning, and to his converting a heavier metal-turning lathe for turning wood.
Kai enjoys woodworking and woodturning as a spare-time activity which, thanks to magazines like *Woodturning* and many English books on the subject, also allows him to brush up his English.
He is 33 years old and is married with a young son.

Photo 9 *Now the top is rounded. Note the fingernail-shaped gouge.*

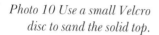

Photo 10 *Use a small Velcro disc to sand the solid top.*

Photo 11 *Turn a wooden cone to fit the top hole.*

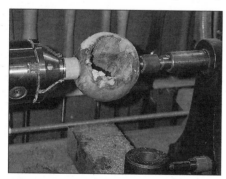

Photo 12 *Remount the workpiece.*

Photo 13 *The supporting cone can be removed with a 60 grit Velcro disc held in a chuck.*

At this stage, little defects in the wood can still be repaired using cyanoacrylate glue (Super glue).

Now remove the tailstock and round the top. I use a hand-held drill and a shallow spindle gouge ground to a long fingernail shape to finish the top (Photo 9).

A small Velcro disc can be used to sand the solid top (Photo 10), but don't Velcro-sand the hollow part, as there's a danger of catching the disc and ruining the piece.

Next, you have to turn a wooden cone that fits the top hole (Photo 11) before re-mounting the workpiece on the lathe (Photo 12). The bottom can now be turned and sanded.

Although this is standard practice in bowl turning, here there's a danger of losing the workpiece because of rotten wood.

Attempting a finishing cut across the whole bottom when the supporting cone in the middle has already been turned quite thin is hazardous. It's much safer to finish the outer areas first and progress towards the middle, reducing the centre cone to a small diameter just before you stop the lathe.

The cone can either be removed totally using a 60 grit Velcro disc held in a drill chuck mounted at the spindlestock end or by cutting it off carefully and finishing by sanding (Photo 13).

Final treatment

With half-rotten wood there's always the danger the wood might be inhabited by unwanted livestock, or that fungus might spread. Both can easily be treated by placing the finished weed pot in a microwave oven set at defrost for 2 or 3 minutes. Allow it to cool, then repeat the procedure.

If the wood is overheated, it will begin to burn or char from the inside and you might not notice it – so take care. Note that wet wood can deform when microwaved.

After microwaving, I treat the finished surface with oil. Clean your workshop carefully, because some insects which live in rotten wood might like to get to work on your carefully selected and stored wood as much as you do.

Safety

Always wear a plexiglass face shield when there is a possibility of small pieces of rotten wood flying off the lathe. A face mask or an air stream helmet is advisable when sanding, because fungus in rotten wood can be hazardous.

When you stop the lathe to check your work, you should also check whether it's held safely. ∎

TURNING BIG

ERNIE CONOVER

Low speed and good basic joinery is all it takes to turn columns says Ernie.

My venture into large turning really started with my wife Susan deciding we needed a new porch. This turned into three porches — a front porch, a side porch and a screen porch in the rear. It was as if I went shopping for a Mini Cooper and ended up buying a Rolls Royce.

Our first thought was to make Victorian-style porches which would incorporate a lot of turning. After much debate, we contacted an architect, which is what we should have done in the first place! He advised us to do the front and side porches in Greek Revival style which is typical of this part of Ohio and would make our rather modern house unique without it becoming hackneyed.

The architect, knowing I was a turner, designed the front and side porches around five large Grecian columns. As you can see from my drawing the main part of each column is 305mm 12" just above the plinth and tapers to 235mm 9¼" just

Ernie Conover is our contributing editor in America. He teaches woodworking in general, and woodturning in particular, at Conover Workshops, a school he and his wife Susan operate together. In addition to writing and lecturing widely, he is a technical consultant to a number of companies on design and manufacture of woodworking tools and machines.

under the capital. Each column sits on a 405mm 16″ square plinth and is topped by a 355mm 14″ capital.

While we built the porches over the next year I spent my spare time researching how large columns were turned years ago. Our columns may look big to modern eyes but they pale in scale to those turned in yesteryear. A building in a town nearby has columns that are 1.8m 6′ DIA at the base and about 9.1m 30′ high. They are coopered and turned in one piece exclusive of plinths and capitals.

My friend Burt Thompson in Ontario, Canada, sent me a photo of he and his father lying inside a column they turned in their shop in the early 1920s.

My year of study found that most of the big Greek columns were coopered, often with the staves being tapered to conserve wood and time in turning. While such construction at first seems baffling it would be well within the ability of any cooper.

Glues

Old columns were glued with a number of waterproof glues, including casein glues. An old recipe for a waterproof glue was to soften Scotch (hide) glue in water. It was then boiled in an iron pot with linseed oil until a good glue was formed. Borax was added to prevent putrefaction.

After the porches had been held up for something over a year on five 100mm x 100mm 4″ x 4″ timbers, my wife Susan shocked me one day. She presented me with a quote from a company in Pittsburgh, Pennsylvania who would make the columns for $575 each. She announced that if columns were not in place by the end of the month. she was going to order them from Pittsburgh.

My Scots blood boiled and I headed for the turning shop. Seeing as I was now under some urgent time constraints, I

decided to have a local cabinetmaker, Christ Miller, do the actual stock preparation and gluing up.

Some calculations showed that by coopering to 12 sides I did not have to taper the joints. This allowed simple construction with straight cuts in the table saw (FIG 1). Christ elected to use three biscuit joints between each stave to make alignment during glue-up easier. Lacking a biscuit jointer, dowels would work just as well. He spread more than enough glue with a small paint roller and drew each column together with three band clamps. As extra insurance Christ drove air staples at the ends.

Christ used a waterproof sigh glue called Ultra Bond. The same glue is now generally available from Tightbond as their Type II glue. It is a PVA (poly vinyl acetate) formula with additives to make it water resistant. The time-honoured plastic resin glues (formalde-hyde urea resin) that you mix with water would work just as well. Either glue will work fine but the advantage of Tightbond

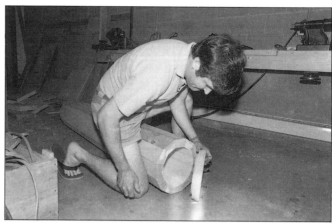

Photo 1 Fitting one of the tapered end plugs into one end of the column. It was screwed into place.

or batten, between the two bed planks which were 50mm x 150mm 2″ x 6″. To this tongue I bolted another 1.5m 5′ of bed rail. I then drilled and bolted the leg to the new end which gave me the requisite 2.4m 8′ between centres.

I allowed the bed to overhang each end leg a good 460mm 18″ so I could place hydraulic jacks at these points. I then put 100mm x 100mm 4″ x 4″ posts between my jacks and the ceiling rafters of my shop. I then 'jacked' my lathe down onto the floor and figured it would not be going anywhere with my columns because it had the house sitting on it.

Photo 2 Lifting the columns on to the lathe was a two-man job. Not the safest of footwear!

Type II is that it is premixed. I don't recommend epoxies because they are very messy, tough to execute, expensive and completely unnecessary.

While Christ was coopering, I set about doing a stretch job on my lathe. I removed the right hand leg and bolted a tongue,

Since the set-up was temporary this was easier than trying to bolt it to the concrete and created no lasting damage.

Once Christ delivered the glued-up sections, I set about mounting them in the lathe. To do this I turned up two tapered plugs that were a press fit with

the inside of the columns. One I left mounted on the faceplate used for turning and the other I centre drilled 10mm ⅜″. Using a wooden mallet I tapped these into the end of each column and secured them in place with four dry wall or self tapping screws (Photo 1). ▶

FIG 1 The basis of the column is a cylinder coopered from 12 staves.

End cap with faceplate provides positive drive.

Special live centre with 10mm ⅜″ core point. Core point is a dowel pin which engages in a drilled hole in the end cap.

Hoisting into the lathe was a two-person job. One person would catch the 10mm ⅜" hole with a special ball bearing (live) centre and keep things there while the other threaded the faceplate to the spindle (Photo 2).

The special tailstock centre is a 10mm ⅜" steel dowel pin that fits into a drilled hole of the same size. It can take the heavy radial loads much better

FIG 2 The turned column with entasis taper.

355mm
14"

50mm
2"
100mm
4"

Capital

235mm
9¼"

305mm
12"

276mm
10⅞"

305mm
12"

286mm
11¼"

305mm
12"

300mm
11¾"

305mm
12"

305mm
12"

305mm
12"

305mm
12"

305mm
12"

100mm
4"
50mm
2"

Plinth

405mm
16"

and, more importantly, the work cannot slip out of the lathe if the tailstock ram works loose.

Actual turning was straightforward. Rough turning was done at 200 RPM while finishing was done at 350 RPM. I used a 610mm 24" rest, but if I had it to do over again I would weld up a 915mm 36" or longer model

out of structural steel.

Spindle turning of this dimension requires large tools with large handles. I used a 32mm 1¼" roughing gouge with a 460mm 18" handle and a skew of similar proportions. A large skew is really necessary if you are to avoid the heel and toe from constantly digging in. The bigger the better — 50mm 2" or 75mm 3" if you can find one (Photos 3 and 4).

I roughed the column to basic shape with the roughing gouge taking calliper readings every foot. I then smoothed up and finalised the taper with the skew. Power sanding to 180 grit with an auto body type rubber disc sander (again with the work turning in the lathe) resulted in a finished column ready for primer (FIG 2).

My first column was not the finest work I have ever done, but nothing plastic wood and epoxy mixed with wood shavings couldn't cure. I put it in the least visible place but oddly I seem to be the only one who notices anything wrong with it.

Symmetrical

It is my belief that the human eye makes things symmetrical, even if they are not. The unwritten assignment to the viewer is, "forgive this poor turner and make these things look alike." The other four turned out just fine and each was in and out of the lathe in about 45 minutes.

Once the columns were turned I set about turning the large bead just above the plinths and the flair just under the capitals. For these I used white pine and held them on faceplates. For alignment I turned a spigot that was a loose fit with the inside of the column and drilled a 12mm ½" hole in the centre for dowelling to the adjacent square.

I primed and painted everything before installation, even rolling primer on the inside of the columns. With a small hydraulic jack I lifted the porch

Photo 3 Starting the turning. Note the vertical beam pressing the lathe bed to the floor.

Photo 4 Using a large gouge for the inital rough shaping.

slightly and knocked out the temporary 100mm x 100mm 4" x 4" braces. Then it was just a matter of sliding the assembled column into place, levelling it up and releasing the jack. Hey presto – my mundane back porch was transformed into a temple of leisure.

At installation my thought was to seal the column as much as possible. As noted above I primed the inside and caulked the assembled unit so that it was virtually hermetically sealed. This was unwise and I found that the column swelled and contracted unduly.

I have found that all the old columns were vented, and so I have now vented mine. Small aluminium vent screens (exactly like the galvanised steel ones I have observed in old columns) are available at good timber yards and DIY stores. One should be installed near the top and one near the bottom on the least weathered side. Fortunately this is usually the least visible side too.

The Confounder ■

> "I jacked my lathe down onto the floor and figured it would not be going anywhere with my columns because it had the house sitting on it."

P PROJECT

MICHAEL SEISER

Michael Seiser began woodturning 40 years ago with a training class project – a darning egg.
This, for the benefit of younger readers, was a wooden egg inserted into a sock which was used as a form around which the sock could be darned.
Michael was born and educated in New Jersey on the USA's eastern seaboard. He became interested in teaching woodworking, and attended a New Jersey State college, majoring in Industrial Arts Education.
He was awarded a Bachelor of Science degree in education and later a Master of Arts.
A high school teacher for 28 years, he left to set up in business as a furniture maker, founding Shaker Furniture of Cape Cod,

Lace bobbins are a good exercise in the fine art of turning, giving both hobbyist and production turner the chance to show off their skills and creativity – and to boost their profits. In the first of two articles on bobbins, we look at basic tools and techniques.

Mini marvels

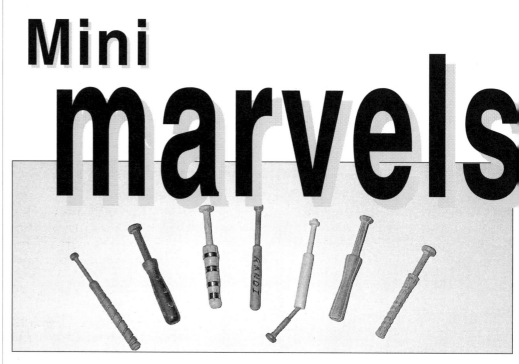

A selection of bobbins (left to right): leopard, tiger, personalized, cow-in-calf, inlaid and grooved.

located in Wellfleet, Massachusetts. It's a job he continues to do.
Michael became interested in lace bobbins and small lathe work through an aunt whose hobby was lacemaking.
He finds bobbins challenging to make and a good way to sharpen skills as a precision lathe operator.
Michael has written articles for several woodworking journals in the USA. This is his first writing venture in the UK.

A full-size lathe is used to rough turn production bobbins. A steady rest and two rest bases are used for support and speed.

What are lace bobbins and why would I want to make them? This was my initial reaction when asked to turn these delicate objects, and you probably had similar thoughts when you read the subject of this article.

So let me start by defining them. A lace bobbin is a finely turned object used by the lacemaker in large quantities to store the thread while making lace.

Now for the second part of the answer. The lace bobbin can offer both production and hobby woodturners the chance to show off their skills on small objects and to create a new market for their work.

The profit potential is high. A fancy piece of lace needs up to 1,000 bobbins, while the speciality bobbin will find a ready market in the collectors' world.

So your scrap hardwoods can literally be crafted into buck-a-minute collectors' items. The technique of turning them calls for some practice, the emphasis being on speed and precision.

A lace bobbin is small. Average length is 90mm-100mm 3 ½"-4" and they are usually about as thick as a pencil. The main concern in turning things this slender is that they will flex over the nose of the tool and break.

You will need to develop a 'touch' for thin work. Scaling the lathe and cutting tools to the size of the job helps –

miniatures for miniatures. I use a modelmaker's or jeweller's lathe made by Unimat and grind my own tools.

I fashion them from old chisels, files and lathe tools. My favourite was made from a 12mm 1/2" gouge, sharpened so many times the blade is now about 100mm 4" long. The long handle and the short blade make it most comfortable to use.

So is my three-jaw chuck. Collets, drive sockets and probably even a Jacob's chuck would be faster, but I'm used to the three-jaw. You should experiment – try all the methods, then pick and stick with the one that's right for you.

Mastering the techniques

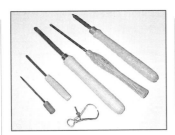

My tools (left to right): home-made roundnose, gouge, customised roundnose, gouge and parting tool.

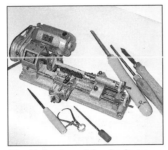

The Unimat modelmaker's or jeweller's lathe.

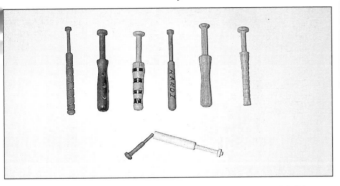

Bobbins (left to right): spiral, leopard, tiger, personalized, inlaid, grooved, bottom and cow-in-calf.

won't take long if you have done any turning at all, and a full-sized lathe will do the job as well as the little guy shown here.

Miniature lathe turning basically incorporates the same basic procedures used in traditional full-sized spindle turning, but on a smaller scale.

Preparing the wood is the same as for bigger projects, with pieces glued to provide a blank of the right size and wood types. Mixed woods and limitations are often used in bobbin turning.

The edges of the prepared billet are planed off to avoid splitting, which commonly occurs in small scale turning. It can be avoided by using only very sharp tools and cutting

The turning position

with a light, controlled touch.

Mounting the blank on the mini-lathe is the same as for a larger lathe. I like to cut the live centre end of the wood with a back saw before setting the spur by gently tapping with a mallet.

The dead centre is also set with a mallet tap. Special attention is given to toolrest position, which should be set so the tool is positioned at a spot just

above centre.

The small diameter of the turning necessitates that the tool, not the steady rest, be placed at the above centre position. Sharp tools, often ground by the bobbin maker, are handled with a gentle touch.

Tool control can best be mastered by practice. Every turner has favourite tools for certain jobs. Carry these preferences with you when making the step from large to small – scale lathe work.

When rough cutting to round, I use a 1/4" gouge ground down to a shaft length of about 100mm 4", but which still retains its full-sized handle.

Smoothing and roughing out to basic shape is done with a round nosed tool ground from drill stock and stuck in a little dowel handle.

Other home-made tools are used for details, but my basic tools are the gouge and the round nose. Sandpaper shaping is largely used in the final process, with grades ranging from 80 to 220.

Finishing is best done on the lathe, using a French polish, tung oil, or urethane. At least five coats are applied. Between each one, steel wool with quad zero abrasive is used. Several coats of wax complete the operation.

Once the operator becomes proficient in the cutting process, many bobbins can be produced in an hour.

A good source of design ideas is *Lace and Lacemaking* by Alice-Mary Bullock (Carousse & Co, 1981, New York).

Perhaps you now feel confident enough to get fancy. So how about doing an inlay, perhaps a leopard, tiger, or cow-in-calf, all traditional types of lace bobbins.

The inlay is self-explanatory. Different types of wood are used in construction, sometimes laminated, but more

often inlaid into the surface. I like to do the uncommon, so most of my wood combinations are laminated or spliced.

As leopards have spots and tigers stripes, so do the bobbins named after them. Holes drilled through the leopard bobbin and grooves turned in tiger bobbins are filled with pewter.

Where do you get pewter? Well, pewter is an alloy containing at least half of tin. My plumbing supply store sells it in wire and bar form.

The traditional way to apply the pewter to the bobbin was to use a mould. The bobbin was rough turned, and grooves were cut or holes drilled for the pewter to flow into.

MOULD

The bobbin was placed in the stone or plaster mould and the molten pewter poured in. The bobbin was then remounted on the lathe and finish turned.

Since pewter solders so easily, I use that method. Pounding the wire pewter flat and to the width of the groove I have turned, I wrap it around the bobbin and apply heat at the joint. Finish turning completes the tiger.

A leopard is even easier. Drill a hole, cut pewter wire to length, bend and shape over and finish turn. The only potential problem is pewter dust showing up in the wood grain. Careful sanding eliminates this.

The cow-in-calf is a novelty bobbin needing precision turning. The small 'calf' bobbin must friction fit into the 'mother.'

In the 18th century, a bobbin maker would travel from town to town making his living with his foot-powered lathe. You too can make a few spare-time dollars by making them from scrapwood.

But the most satisfying aspect of bobbin making is the diversity and creativity it gives to woodturners within a simple and fundamental craft. ●

Göran Sätterström, 51, lives in the south of Sweden, near the Baltic town of Karlskrona, which hit the headlines in 1981 when a Russian submarine was stranded just outside it.
He works as a full-time consultant in soil mechanics and foundation engineering.
Göran's interest in wood goes back to his early childhood, when his father and a neighbour taught him to turn on an old cast-iron lathe.

Close-up of the mug holder *(above)*.

The coffee mug holders in place on the company's lunchroom wall *(left)*.

WHAT A MUG!

GÖRAN SÄTTERSTRÖM

When Swedish amateur woodturner Göran Sätterström agreed to make 30 'artistic' coffee mug holders for the works lunchroom wall, he little realised the sleepless nights and family ridicule it would cause him.

He doesn't see himself as a master turner, rather someone who gets "a lot of more or less crazy ideas" which he tries to realise on the lathe. Most of the ideas, he says, are too crazy and end up in total disaster. "But if you don't fail you don't learn." In his turning, he tries to adjust the form to the type of wood being used. A big bowl in delicate cherry should be rather thin with a smooth form, he says, while a bowl in Swedish pine can be rough in form. Göran adds that the turning point in his turning came when he discovered English books on the subject. In Sweden, he says, there is just one book worthy of the name of woodturning literature. He is convinced a lot of Swedish woodturners would welcome the translation of English books.

It began at lunch two months ago, when our secretary burst into the lunchroom. "Ooh, this room is a mess," she told my colleagues and I. "It's dull, grey, dirty and there are dirty coffee mugs all over the place. We must do something to make it cosy."

I agreed, and suggested we asked our boss for money to buy new furniture, curtains and so on.

"I'm afraid there's no cosymoney left," she said. "We'll have to fix it ourselves. Why don't we get together a few evenings after work to freshen it up?

"I can sew new curtains, you can paint the walls, you can do this, you can do that," and so on. "Göran, you *will* make some nice hooks for all those coffee mugs, won't you? Something artistic."

Before I knew what I was doing, I had agreed.

"Good," she said. "Have them ready in about three weeks. Then we'll have an opening party for the new lunchroom."

Well, how do you turn an 'artistic' holder for 30 coffee mugs? Thirty knobs on a wall, perhaps? Is that artistic? No, it isn't. And besides, turning 30 knobs all the same! No, it's definitely not 'artistic' enough.

Days and sleepless nights went by and the problem remained unsolved. I couldn't come up with any good ideas. "How's the holder coming along?" I was asked. "Working on it," I replied.

Finally, the answer arrived — one week before the deadline. A child had thrown a plastic toy into an appletree and I saw it hanging nicely on a branchfork. That was it (see FIG 1).

I headed for the woods with secateurs and a plastic bag. Luckily, woodmen had trimmed small bushes and trees, leaving the wood in piles. It

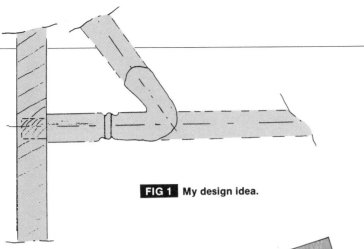

FIG 1 My design idea.

Now I could mount the fork in the cone and support it with the rubber pad. In this way I could slide and move the fork until I found some average centre. I turned the peg to 8mm $5/16$" and recentred the fork for the beadturning.

In some cases, the bent and oval form made it impossible to turn beads without getting the effect shown in FIG 3. In those cases I turned the spindle by hand and simply cut the bead with a sharp skew chisel.

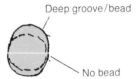

FIG 3 Turning beads is difficult on oval wood.

didn't take me long to get enough forks.

I knew they had to be seasoned before they were glued into the drilled holes, or they would fall out when the wood shrank. Perhaps the microwave could help?

I was alone in the house that night, so I loaded the microwave with forks and dried them in two minute cycles with a cooling period between.

But my luck ran out — my wife and son came home. My son, hungry as usual, realised the microwave was on. "Is supper ready, Dad?" he asked. "It smells delicious."

He opened the microwave and stared in disbelief. "Mum, come and help me with Dad," he cried. "We must get him to hospital and have his brain examined. His interest in wood has passed the limit — now he's going to eat it."

I tried to explain what I was doing in a scientific way, but they didn't understand. They just laughed and said I was crazy. Well, maybe I am a bit crazy, but a crazy man gets crazy ideas, and crazy ideas sometimes turn out well.

Anyway, the seasoning worked a treat, although it took some time. The bark stopped the moisture evaporating, I suppose. I returned to my workshop to turn the pegs and maybe a bead or two.

I intended to mount the forks in my three-jaw chuck and turn them. But that didn't work because branchforks don't know they are meant to be round and straight, preferring to be oval and shaped like a bow.

To overcome this problem, I mounted a piece of wood in the screwchuck and turned a cone-shaped hole in it. On the revolving tailstock I mounted a flat piece with a soft rubber pad glued to it (FIG 2).

Now I had 30, rather good, hooks to be mounted on some sort of board. I mounted a few on an ordinary board, but it was disastrous.

Close to panic, I scoured my stock of wood, but could not find the right thing. I thought of giving the hooks to that *?/! secretary and telling her to do what she liked with them.

In a last ditch effort I dived behind my workbench, and found a well seasoned log of blue-spalted pine. I cut off a slice and, eureka, there was my first base.

I cut the log into 10mm $3/8$" thick slices, drilled a hole exactly in the pith centre and mounted the hooks. I glued and screwed (from the back) the slices to a small, thin strip of wood.

There it was — the 'artistic' turned coffee mug holder. Or was it? What is artistic, anyway? You can judge for yourself from the photos. This type of hook can, of course, be used for other purposes than coffee mugs.

Every turner must be asked now and then to make something special. But I think I must be the only one who has ever been asked to turn 30 'artistic' coffee mug holders for a company's lunchroom.

They even kept the secretary quiet — for a while. ∎

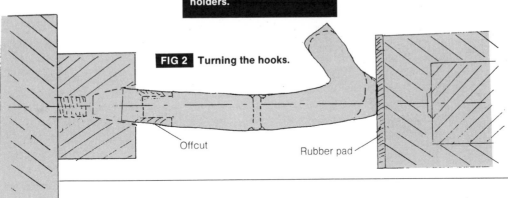

The 'artistic' coffee mug holders.

FIG 2 Turning the hooks.

Offcut

Rubber pad

Two seater settee, oak, with natural seagrass seating, seat height approx. 305mm, 12".

'I look to ethnic and Indian furniture for inspiration, and also to architecture – towers and spires'.

FIT FOR A VICEROY

Armchair, poplar, with coir seating, seat height approx. 200mm, 8", hand woven cushion in cotton.

Neil Bousfield specialises in making Indian-style throne chairs, for which Clair Randell weaves the seats. Nigel Gardner describes what turns them on to these viceregal creations.

To call Neil Bousfield's turned creations "chairs", is a bit like calling the Taj Mahal a "tomb", or the Red Fort palace a "house". They are more like "thrones", fit for a maharajah, viceroy, or even a mogul emperor.

"I look to ethnic and Indian furniture for inspiration, and also to architecture – towers and spires", said Neil. "I like crude, basic work and wood that has a roughness to it. For me, it seems to be more natural".

This is why he uses sandpaper as little as possible, feeling it makes people admire the wood rather than the form. One of the most difficult things in woodwork, he says, is working with a visually powerful material like wood.

Neil, 27, started turning more than two years ago, when he was unemployed. He'd previously worked as a freelance animator for films and tv titles, following an art and design education.

During a brief power cut, he and his 28-year-old partner Clair Randell, decided some candlesticks were in order. But, rather than buy them they decided to get a cheap Taiwanese lathe and make some .

This led to making more furniture, slightly more refined than the first efforts, using more turned parts and developing joinery techniques. Each chair was better than the last and was a development from it.

After six months of turning, Neil thought he was getting the hang of things, so he went to see Reg Sherwin, who refined and improved his skills.

He then bought a Wadkin RS woodturning lathe for £450, a good, heavy, three-phase machine, onto which he only had to put a plug. Neil extended the lathe's bed, so it now has 8'6" between centres.

He also put a light pillar drill on the lathe, for which he made a metal clamping plate. This means that, used with an index plate he made, Neil can accurately and easily drill holes around the circumference and at any position, on large, turned spindles.

The lathe also came with a geared carriage as well as a free standing rest. So, Neil made an adaptor plate for the carriage, allowing him to fit his router onto the lathe and cut mortises as accurately as he can drill holes.

This helps him a lot with making large chairs and beds, the work he likes to do. Neil makes dining chairs as well as a lower, armchair style.

"I'd like to develop them more and try for a cleaner, less cluttered style of turning", he said. "I'd also like to make them more sculptural and bigger, perhaps for outdoor sites".

Neil says it's impossible not to be influenced by other turners, but finds it difficult to name them, though he particularly likes the work of Mike Scott and Rose-Marie Yeh. They have especially influenced his bowl and vessel turning work.

Bowl, beech, about 230mm, 9" H x 255mm, 10" DIA.

▶

Turned sculpture, scorched black and natural beech and oak, 510mm, 20" DIA x 760mm, 30" L approx.

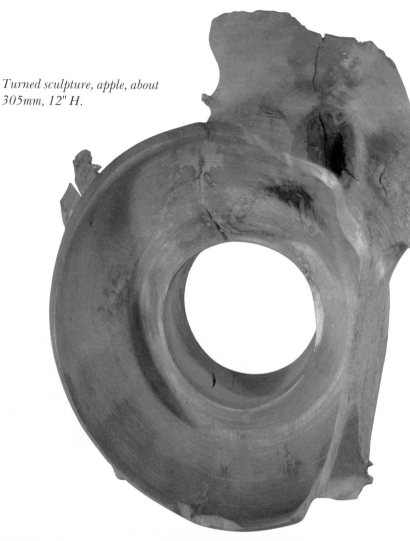

Turned sculpture, apple, about 305mm, 12" H.

"I try to draw on a wide variety of disciplines for inspiration and look to sculpture for a purer form", he said.

He has built several large chairs from wet oak, including the rails, but has also made one in dry poplar and another in dry beech, with kiln-dried ash rails.

His best results have been with 125mm, 5" section oak legs, using dry ash rails. They're joined with a 38mm, 1 ½" DIA tenon, 50mm, 2" long; sometimes these are sawn down the middle about 38mm, 1 ½" for wedges, sometimes two small coves are turned onto the tenon so that the tenon can be pegged in place with 10mm, ⅜" kiln-dried beech dowel.

"I like to use wet oak, as it's easily obtainable in large, square sections, ready to turn", he said. "I also like the way wet wood warps, cracks and splits".

His large, wet, pieces of oak, full of knots, are rough turned and left in the warm for about six weeks to split and warp, before re-turning and assembling.

Massive bed

An early project, as a professional, was a massive bed containing 18 cu ft of timber, with four turnings of 150mm, 6" DIA, some 2m, 6'6" long.

At the time of writing he had just finished turning 42 bowls over two weeks, ranging from 305mm, 12" to 510mm, 20" DIA, and from 125mm, 5" to about 125mm, 12" deep

Most have ribs, beads and coves cut into them, and will be scorched, wire brushed and textured. But Neil is also interested in colouring wood and in using metal, especially copper, to pin the splits.

As he had to turn these pieces about 180mm, 7" away from the rest, with a standard bowl gouge, he found the hollowing work pushed him to his limits. He didn't want to sand them, so had to work hard to improve his turning technique.

This, he feels, he achieved, and most of the pieces bear no trace of a centre, with few ridges and tool marks.

As he turns a foot on a bowl, which he likes to be chunky, with a bit of weight on it, he doesn't have to worry about faceplate screws.

But chairs are his first love. These are made on spec, in a small farm outbuilding.

Double bed, in oak, with oak slats. All four legs are 2m, 6'6" tall, 150mm, 6" section.

Assembly takes place in the garden, or front room. The biggest so far produced has a 2.4m, 8ft back leg.

They take about three days to turn and another three or four to have their seagrass seats woven. This, and the weaving of cushion covers, is done by Clair, who has a BA Hons in Woven Textiles.

"We have both had an interest in building larger items of work", she said, "drawing influences from castles we have visited around Britain and by looking at the construction of timber-framed buildings.

"From this we began making crude attempts of some basic stools and tables for our own use, utilising some of the construction methods (using wooden dowels) and the simple styles.

"Making chairs seemed a good opportunity to combine our skills of woodturning and

Single bed, oak, scorched black, the two back legs 2.7m, 7' tall.

Walnut candlesticks.

weaving. We both contribute to the designs and in assembling each piece of furniture".

Clair first tried to weave a strong seat by using coir twine from the garden centre. This was woven in blocks, giving a supportive and strong seat, but it was "incredibly scratchy". She then discovered seagrass, which is now used for all the chairs.

"In the cushion covers I have woven so far, I have used fairly thick yarns to achieve a substantial looking fabric which complements the style and scale of our chairs", she said.

Her influences are mixed, with inspiration drawn from architecture, medieval buildings in particular, and also from travels in Turkey, North America and Mexico.

"I am also influenced by African and Indian art and textiles", she said, "although I have not visited these countries yet". ∎

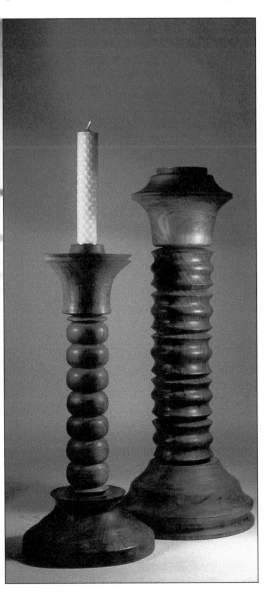

BACK TO WORK

Reg decides it's time to get another project on the go, in case readers think he has sold his lathe.

Looking back through my recent columns, I see it's some time since I was actually seen to be making something for sale rather than just creating an EEC shavings mountain.

Before readers start wondering whether I've sold my lathes and tools, or forgotten how to turn, let me get a project on the go, albeit a basic one.

Being a 'jobbing' turner, I never know what's coming through the workshop door next.

Recently, a man brought a broken chair into the workshop, whose front stretcher was deficient in three important areas – design, material and solidity.

The 32mm, 1 ¼" DIA stretcher had a cove strategically placed right at the centre of its 410mm, 16" length. But the cheap mahogany had not been able to withstand the robust behaviour of some miscreant and had 'come from together' as my old dad used to say.

Head stuck

I had been involved in a similar situation myself, when young. I was about eight at the time and, taking an interest in wood, somehow managed to get my head stuck between the stretchers of an old dining chair.

My grandfather rescued me, but not before he filled my young mind with thoughts of having to go to school the next day with the new adornment, because he "couldn't find his saw".

Anyway, I was now rectifying rather than causing the kerfuffle, and suggested to the stretcher bearer that a more

suitable timber for the job might be beech, which he could stain. I also suggested a better central design and a price.

The result was I now had yet another fill-in job, albeit a rather urgent one, as the chair's front legs were starting to splay.

The first job was to put the sawn blank of straight grained beech between centres and turn it down to a cylinder.

Longer

As the wood is longer than the toolrest, and also comparatively narrow, I tend to start at the headstock end of the lathe and produce a cylinder with my small roughing gouge (see above left photo).

Notice the steps on the wood to the right of the tool? This is to avoid the possibility of the tool rolling over to the right when its wing touches the area where the previous cut finished.

Also notice the presentation of the tool to the wood. I find that using this method of allowing the wood to come onto the cutting edge of the tool at 90 DEG, and stopping short of the previous cut each time, I can get down to a cylinder very quickly.

If the wood is shorter than the toolrest, of course, I can go right off the end of the wood and back again.

To clean up the part of the surface which is likely to show on the finished piece, I use a shearing cut with the lower wing of the same roughing gouge. Once again, the tool is supported down the shaft from the area which is cutting, and is therefore unlikely to roll.

Above left: The first job is to put the sawn blank between centres and turn it to a cylinder, using a small roughing gouge at a 90 DEG angle to the wood.

Above: A shearing cut is made with the lower wing of the same roughing gouge.

Below: Cutting a chamfer with a beading tool.

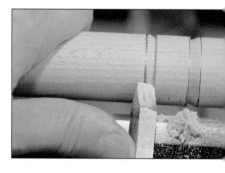

The rest of the square blank is now rounded in stages, using the 90 DEG cut. The left hand supporting the revolving wood reduces its tendency to 'whip'.

I cut the chamfers with a beading tool after the work has been marked out. This cut is almost identical to stage one of the pummel cut shown in Chapter 10 of *The Practical Woodturner* by Frank Pain.

Again, note the left hand supporting the revolving timber. If you smell pork, let go.

The central portion is shaped into a bead. In the photo, the right side is waiting for final blending in with the left which is receiving its first cut.

For the second cut, the tool is rolled over to the left while its handle is arced

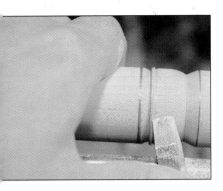

...tarting to shape the bead of the central ...ortion.

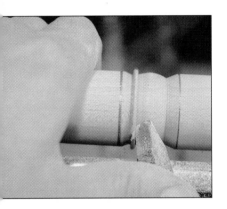

Here, the bead is almost complete.

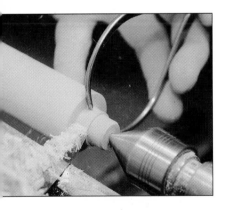

A beading tool and callipers are used to ...ize the tenon which fits into the chair leg.

...ound to the right. The final stage is to ...lean up and make it symmetrical.

A beading tool and callipers are used to ...roduce the round tenon at the end of ...he stretcher, which is to fit into the hole ...n the chair leg.

I soften the callipers' sharp ends with a ...lip stone, to reduce the chance of a catch.

The beading tool is arced down, cut-...ing the wood, rather than being pushed ...orward in a scraping action. This arcing ...path gives more control to the cut and a

The finished tenon with rounded shoulder reversed into the ring drive.

The hand supports the wood, while the thumb supports the tool.

Sanding is done with the vacuum cleaner nozzle clipped over the top of the toolrest.

longer life to the tool's cutting edge.

Next I put a radius on the shoulder of the stretcher where the tenon starts. A radius is like half a bead and this one was done with the beading tool, 'cos I had it in my hand.

As I'm driving the work from a ring drive centre, I can turn the work end for end and use the chamfer to locate inside the cone of the drive centre.

The other end of the stretcher, now at the tailstock end of the lathe, is now sized

The stretcher now has a much more suitable central feature.

and radiused, and the general shaping completed.

The hand supports the wood, the thumb supports the tool. Keep the bevel in contact with the wood, as it has been in all of the cuts so far.

The first sanding operation is done with 180 grit cloth. The vacuum cleaner nozzle is clipped over the top of the tool-rest to take in the dust.

As a different part of the work is sand-ed, so the nozzle moves along the rest, or the rest is moved along the lathe bed.

After the 180 grit sanding, the work-piece is again turned end for end between centres and quickly sanded with 220 grit. This sanding gets rid of the few small fibres which have bent back rather than been cut off during the first sanding.

The fact that the timber is now revolv-ing in the opposite direction helps this operation a lot.

All that remains is for the customer to play around with the stain on the couple of smaller pieces of beech I turned for him at the same time, so he can get the colour right before committing himself to the replacement part. ∎

The author

Reg Sherwin is Woodturning's UK Contributing Editor. He began woodturning in 1966, starting with a power drill attachment. Reg has a workshop at the Avoncroft Museum of Buildings at Bromsgrove, West Midlands, where he teaches and demonstrates on open days

Thimble thrift

Today's timber prices, not to mention conservation, make it essential to use every scrap of wood. This thimble project by Bill Nairn shows how even the smallest piece of waste can be turned into something attractive and useful.

Thimbles are an interesting way to use up small scraps of wood around the workshop.

Any type of wood can be used, but one which is fine-grained, like purple heart, yew, kingwood or ebony, is best. You can use a coarse-grained wood, such as oak, but the wall has to be made slightly thicker.

The first thing to consider is how to hold the wood, as we need to turn both the inside and outside of the thimbles. A small screw chuck works well, while a four-jaw chuck is ideal.

If you only want the thimbles for display, a ½" pin chuck is also good, as you can complete the outside on the pin chuck and leave the inside as a straight hole.

For small pieces, a knock-in or a glue-on chuck is effective. I now use a ½" Jacobs chuck for most of my thimbles, tending to make a small batch at one go. I complete them all at one stage before moving on to the next, rather than finishing them one at a time.

Select a few blocks of wood about 30mm, 1 ⅛" square by 50mm, 2" long and mount between centres. Turn down to about 25mm 1" DIA with a roughing gouge, then reduce one end to 12mm ½" to fit in the chuck for about half its length.

When all the blanks have been roughed out in this way, attach your chuck to the lathe and then fit the first of the cylinders into it.

Set the lathe to 2000 RPM (if not already at this speed) and, with a light cut, true up the blank. Now mark the blank for the length of the thimble, using a parting tool with callipers to set the three diameters.

Cut to size

Cut the taper down to size with a ¼", 6mm gouge or small skew chisel, as you prefer. Decide how you want the large end to look (straight taper, coved, or the more normal beaded), then turn as required.

Start to remove the waste wood at the chuck end and to form the thimble top, leaving about 6mm, ¼" of a stem at this stage. Now for the delicate part:

hollowing out the centre.

I usually start this by using a ¼ gouge as a drill. I line up its centre with that of the thimble end, and carefully push in the gouge with a slight side to side movement, to the depth required.

A mark on the gouge, or a piece of tape, helps if you are making a few, as it saves time checking the depth each time.

Widen hole

To widen the hole, I use a ¼" scraper ground both on the end and (for the first 38mm, 1 ½") on the left hand side. It's easy to see the angle required by looking over the top of the thimble.

Make the wall as delicate as you like but remember that coarse-grained woods need a slightly thicker wall than fine-grained.

Sand the inside with a piece of rolled-up sandpaper to the smoothness required, then polish the inside. The outside is finished on a jam-chuck.

To make the jam-chuck, fit a piece of scrap wood to your chuck, and taper it to fit the inside of the thimble, which is mounted for finishing by pushing onto the taper. Turn off the end to make the domed top, using the gouge or screw.

If you want to embellish your thimble, now is the time to do it. Sand and polish. I use a melamine finish, as a

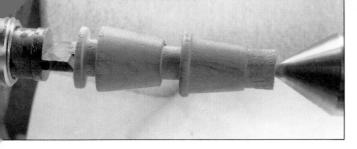

Rough blank, turned between centres. Leave an area at the top of the thimble for gripping in the Jacobs chuck at the next stage.

The thimble held in a Jacobs chuck by the spigot, with the outside turned.

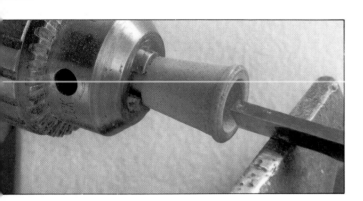

Thimble blank.

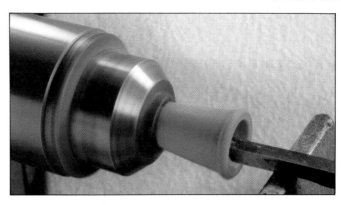

Hollowing the inside.

A scrapwood jam chuck holds the thimble for outside finishing

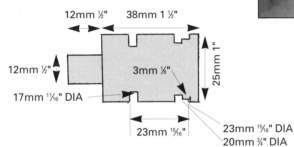

12mm ½"   38mm 1 ½"

12mm ½"
3mm ⅛"
25mm 1"

17mm ¹¹⁄₁₆" DIA

23mm ¹⁵⁄₁₆"

23mm ¹⁵⁄₁₆" DIA
20mm ¾" DIA

Angle approx. 6⁰

The wall thickness depends on the type of wood, but it's about 3mm ⅛"

Working thimbles come in various sizes, to fit different sized fingers. The sizes given here are based on porcelain collectors' thimbles.

hard finish is needed to stand up to the handling thimbles get.

If you want a dimpled top, this can be made by tapping lightly with a small hammer a nail with its point filed off.

Try gluing different types of wood together, to give various patterns. A collection of different types of timber look striking on a display unit.

If you want to include the name of the wood, use a pyrograph iron or

small Letraset rub-on letters.

I hope you'll agree that making thimbles is an attractive way of using waste wood. In the next article (p. 108) I'll show you how to make a stand for them. ■

The finished thimbles.

The author

Bill Nairn, 56, did some turning as part of his apprenticeship as a carpenter and joiner. But it was a visit to a show that sparked off the desire to make it his hobby.
A cheap lathe and one of Gordon Stokes' books helped get him started nearly three years ago. An "excellent" beginners course with Jamie Wallwin at Craft Supplies ironed out some of the snags.
This year, Bill joined the South Manchester Woodturners' Association, Having taken early retirement, he now has more time for turning.

Thimble stand

*The two stands,
without their
glass covering.*

The space between the chuck and the base.

Cutting the groove for the dome with a "spearpoint".

Turning the edge of the base.

Marking the drilling line on one of the 'shelves'.

In his previous article, Bill Nairn described how to make wooden thimbles. Now he describes how to make a glass-domed stand for them.

Now that we have our thimbles (Thimble Thrift, p.106), we need somewhere to display them, and this domed display stand is an ideal way of showing them off to best advantage. I made it for my wife.

There were several design factors to consider. For example, the stand had to hold as many thimbles as possible in relation to its base size. Then, the dust problem had to be eased, so some sort of cover was needed.

Cost was also a factor, as my wife's collection is ever growing and, if I was to make a number of them, the project had to be interesting.

The solution was to use two different sizes of glass domed stands, holding either 29 or 51 thimbles.

I chose to make them in Brazilian mahogany, partly for the colour, as most thimbles look well against it, and partly because of the price.

I should explain that I get this wood cheap from a local window maker, who is only too pleased to let me go through his offcuts. I've picked up many a useful piece cheaply from this source.

Larger stand

As both stands are made in the same way, I give details here for the larger one.

First, as Mrs Beeton would say, obtain your dome. The sizes of these vary, but I use the 100mm 4" x 180mm 7" and the 140mm 5¹/₂" x 280mm 11" ones from Craft Supplies at Buxton, Derbys. It's worth asking if they have a local stockist, as it saves postage.

Plane the base and the shelves to the required thickness with a planer thicknesser. Your timber supplier may do this for you, if you ask nicely. It will suffice off the circular saw, provided

▶

'Cover the base with
stick-on felt, polish the
dome, and present it to
your wife. She's bound to
be impressed, isn't she?'

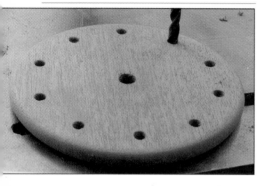

Drilling peg holes.

The completed shelf.

Cutting the centre supports.

*Turning the peg dowel. Note the
supporting finger.*

Thimble holder units

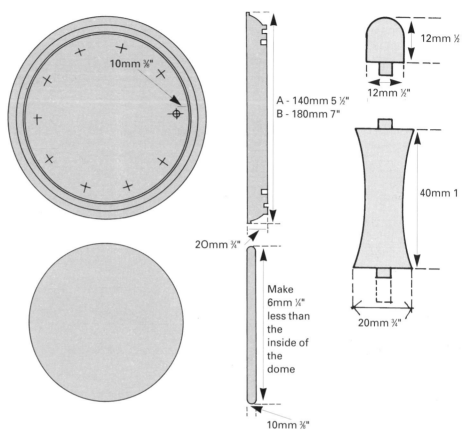

The base is made from wood 140mm 5 ½" or 180mm 7" x 20mm ¾

Make three A shelves and four B, at 6mm ¼" less DIA than the inside of the dome

Three supports are needed for the A shelves and four for the B, at 20mm ¾" DIA, with 40mm 1 ⅝" between shoulders. Make the peg of the bottom one 20mm ¾" long to fit the base

Make 28 pegs for the A shelves and 50 for the B, 20mm ¾" x 6mm ¼" DIA.

Drill seven holes in the A shelves and base, and 10 in the B, 6mm ¼" DIA x 6mm ¼" deep

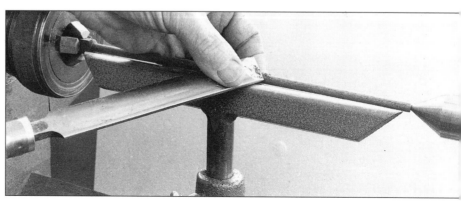

The author

Bill Nairn, 56, was an apprenticed carpenter and joiner with a firm that did everything from rough work to sophisticated jobs for stately homes. Although he did some turning as part of his training, it was a visit to a show which sparked the desire to take it up as a relaxing hobby. A cheap lathe and a Gordon Stokes book helped get him started about three years ago, and an "excellent" beginners course with Jamie Wallwin at Craft Supplies ironed out some of the snags. As there is no turning group where Bill lives, he finds going to the Craft Supplies open days is beneficial, giving him many tips.

The complete holder, ready to take the dome.

you make the rough size a little thicker – it just needs more surfacing in the lathe.

Cut blanks one quarter over size on the bandsaw and bore a hole to fit the screw chuck through each one, as they are to be reversed.

Place packing between the chuck and the base piece, so the screw is covered. Make a light cut with the gouge to level the surface. Hollow it slightly across the face, this being the underside of the base, so the finished stand won't rock.

Sand and finish. I only sand, as I cover the base with green, stick-on felt

to prevent slipping or marking my wife's polished surfaces. I then reverse the disc on the screw chuck and level the face as before. Take the edge down to size and decorate to your choice with a sharp gouge.

Mark out the groove for the glass with the dividers, taking care to only use one point, to avoid a dig. Cut the groove to 5mm ³⁄₁₆" deep, ensuring the fit is not too tight, to allow for timber movement. I use a thin 'spearpoint' for this.

Sand and, with a soft pencil and the lathe running, mark out the centre-line of the holes for the thimble

support pegs. Not having an indexing head on my lathe, I remove the base and mark out the hole centres either directly on the wood using a compass or, if I intend to make a few stands, through the template.

Drill the holes 6mm ¼" DIA x 6mm ¼" deep. Now return the lathe to the base for finishing. I use Melamine, taking care not to get any in the holes or on the first quarter around the centre hole, as this would stop the glue sticking.

Drill the centre hole to 10mm ⅜", slightly countersinking both sides of the hole to prevent the centre support seating badly.

The other shelves are made in the same way. A round edge is easy to do, and looks well.

Plain design

The centre supports are a straight-worward piece of spindle turning, and can be as plain or fancy as you like. I tend to go for a plain design, as I feel it's the thimbles which are on display, not the unit they're displayed in.

If you can hold the timber in a four-jaw chuck, it will help with the parting off. If not, part some way through and finish off with a fine saw after you remove it from the lathe.

Turn enough 6mm ¼" dowels for all the pegs. As in all thin work, it helps to support the work with a finger as you make the final cuts with a skew.

Parting off

I find I can easily handle a 150mm 6" - 230mm 9" length in my four-jaw, with the revolving centre only just revolving, so as not to bend the wood.

After sanding and finishing, part off to 20mm ¾" long and glue in the holes. I find Evo Stik Resin W is fine for most jobs.

Now glue the centre supports and the shelves together, taking care that the shelves are square to the centre supports and vertical to the base.

Cover the base with stick-on felt, polish the dome, and present it to your wife. She's bound to be impressed, isn't she? ∎

DEEP AND DAMP

W.J.PIMLETT

When I was given a newly-felled log of whitebeam by a friend, I thought I would try turning a wooden vase from it. I had already read an article on wet wood turning, and also one by Berle Miller (*Sold on Cedar*) on making wooden vases, in Issue 21 of *Woodturning.*

Working in much the same way as Berle Miller, but using a four-jaw chuck and a centre steady made by my son-in-law,

After reading articles in *Woodturning* on wet wood turning and making wooden vases, W.J.Pimlett decided to have a go himself, and describes how he turned a wet piece of whitebeam into a deep hollowed vase.

Photo 1 Preparing the log on the bandsaw

Photo 8 The finished bowl and vases, waxed and pyrographed. There were no apparent markings on the left hand vase, so the very faint grain was highlighted with the pyrograph tool.

I first trimmed the log on the bandsaw (Photo 1), then turned the log between centres on my Tyme Avon lathe to get a uniform cylinder measuring 405mm 16" x 190mm 7½" DIA, leaving a 25mm 1" stub at one end to fit the four-jaw chuck (Photo 2).

William Pimlett carved his first project – a chess set made from a broom handle – at the age of 12, when he was an evacuee to Colomendy in North Wales.
His only tool was a penknife which, like all boys, he carried in his trouser pocket.
Miniature canoes followed, a source of enjoyment for he and his friends in local streams.
From early days, he says, his first thoughts were, "Can I make it out of wood?"
After leaving school at 14, he had various jobs, including

butchering, until he was called up to do his National Service.
William spent his service time in Egypt, 10 miles from the Great Pyramids, which led to an interest in Egyptology and associated art forms.
After returning to England, he joined the Liverpool City police force, in which he served for 26 years.
While in the police, he took up carving in his spare time and made many carvings of animals including birds and his favourite – dolphins.
William entered a magazine competition for

the carving of a robin on a post, to be made from a single piece of wood. His cherry wood entry won second prize and was shown on the Blue Peter television programme.
On retiring from the police, his wife bought him a lathe, and he now spends a lot of time in the workshop. He says he has been turning for six years and wishes he had started 40 years ago.
Over the years, William has also used watercolours, oils, pastels and charcoal. He enjoys calligraphy, especially Old English script.
He greatly admires the imaginative work of the Australian turners.

Photo 2 Turning to a rough cylinder, leaving a stub on one end to engage the four-jaw chuck.

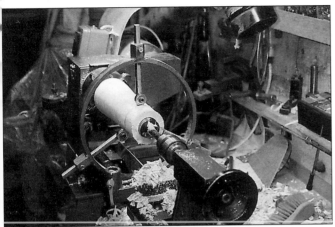

Photo 3 Drill a hole ready for the deep hollowing tool, leaving about 50mm 2" in the base to add weight to the finished vase.

I mounted the cylinder in the four-jaw chuck and brought the centre steady up to about 75mm 3" from the tailstock end and left it loose.

I positioned the tailstock and aligned the cylinder to turn true, tightened the centre steady and removed the tailstock.

I used saw tooth bits and an extension to remove most of the cylinder's inside (Photo 3), then a Deep Adjustable Hollowing Tool (DAHT) to shape it, making the neck about half the diameter of the base (Photo 4). I then sanded and sealed the inside.

When shaping the outside I left a ridge for the centre steady to run on, which was later removed. I used callipers to get an even wall thickness, about 6mm ¼" at this stage.

The base needs to be about 38mm 1½" thick to give weight to the finished vase. I rounded the base off, leaving enough room between it and the four-jaw to part off when the vase was finished.

I next removed the steady centre using the tailstock and a wooden cone to support the vase's neck while trimming off the ridge left for the centre steady. I then sanded the vase to a fine finish.

I marked the stub at the base and numbered it to coincide with the numbers on the four-jaw, as it had now to be removed and returned to the chuck later.

I put the vase in the microwave oven, on as low a setting as possible, and 'cooked' it for two or three minutes, then allowed it to cool.

I repeated this process several times, decreasing the length of drying time. When the damp patch in the centre of the base was just visible, I put the vase in a plastic bag tied at the top.

After a week or so I checked its base to see if the damp patch had gone. If it hadn't, I replaced the vase in the bag for a couple more days until it appeared dry.

At this stage, I returned the vase to the lathe, matching up the numbers on the base stub with the four-jaw (Photos 5,6 and 7). I engaged the wooden cone and tailstock for support and checked the vase was revolving true before sanding,

▶

Photo 5 The vase is returned to the lathe after drying in the microwave. It was given two separate drying times of two minutes on low. Note the widget to help centre the returned vase (an old screwdriver and a piece of dowel).

Photo 4 Using the centre steady and the deep hollowing tool.

Photo 6 A bowl turned, sanded and ready for the microwave oven. The bowl was dried three times for two minutes on the lowest setting of the microwave.

'The vase was placed in the microwave oven, on as low a setting as possible, and "cooked" for two or three minutes, then allowed to cool.'

A selection of bowls and vases, the left two dyed black and enhanced with a 3mm ⅛" carving gouge. The others show how cracks and marks can be used decoratively.

finishing and parting off.

I inspected the piece for hairline cracks, which can be dealt with in several ways. I use a carving gouge to widen or deepen them and a pyrograph to burn in decorative features such as trees, bullrushes, dragonflies and butterflies. Often the tiny cracks will suggest a form. ■

Photo 7 The vase and bowl after drying out in the microwave, ready to be returned to the lathe. Note the tiny crack in the vase and the markings on the bowl, which give rise to the pyrographic work on finished articles.

More of my turnings, some with relief carving and others pyrographed.

Tall vase with dried flowers.

JOHN P. SHERIFF

If you see a man bent double with his ear clamped to a four-foot stick, don't laugh. He will probably be a water engineer using one of Eifion Owen's wooden stethoscopes to listen for leaks.

I t sounds — and looks — comical. But there's nothing funny about the wooden stethoscopes Welshman Eifion Owen turns in his Colwyn Bay workshop. The four-foot stethoscopes are used by skilled engineers to listen for water-pipe leaks underground.

A former REME wireless technician, who later used his metallurgy degree to get a job at

Eifion in his workshop.

EAR TO THE GROUND

a major steelworks, Eifion took up woodturning when he was made redundant.

He first produced full-size furniture in the Welsh village of Caerwys but, after moving to Colwyn Bay, switched to making dolls house furniture.

The stethoscopes, which have an earpiece made from beech, were developed in a joint venture with Vernon Morris, of Chester.

"We had some problems at first," said Eifion. "The main shaft of the stethoscope is a single length of ramin dowel with a slight taper to take a brass ferrule, but the earpiece needs turning. The first few I made had the grain going the wrong way, and were liable to split."

Eifion uses an Arundel lathe with a 4′ 6″ bed and eight speeds. Also a Minicraft drill

with a lathe attachment for a few of his miniatures.

Moving from four-foot stethoscopes to chair legs just 50mm 2″ long is something Eifion takes in his stride. He uses mahogany and ramin for miniature work, as the fine grain is in scale with the small items. His wife, Elizabeth, herself a skilled woodturner, frequently helps.

Eifion's stethoscopes are made for one company, for whom he produces some 200 of the longer models a year. The shorter, pocket version, has a 305mm 12″ shaft, which makes it convenient for carrying about, but must make listening for leaks a back-breaking task.

"The engineers tried swopping to metal stethoscopes," said Eifion, "but one man got blown across the road by an electric shock, so mine are back in demand."

Eifion starts work on a stethoscope earpiece.

It may not be a big enough demand to keep the wolf from the door, but it gives Eifion an unusual use for his turning skills — and as a conversation piece at parties it's hard to beat. ■

Eifion Owen demonstrates the use of his wooden stethoscope.

INDEX

WOODTURNING

Adventures in Woodturning	David Springett	Pleasure & Profit from Woodturning	Reg Sherwin
Bert Marsh: Woodturner	Bert Marsh	Practical Tips for Turners & Carvers	GMC Publications
Bill Jones' Notes from the Turning Shop	Bill Jones	Practical Tips for Woodturners	GMC Publications
Carving on Turning	Chris Pye	Spindle Turning	GMC Publications
Colouring Techniques for Woodturners	Jan Sanders	Turning Miniatures in Wood	John Sainsbury
Decorative Techniques for Woodturners	Hilary Bowen	Turning Wooden Toys	Terry Lawrence
Faceplate Turning: Features, Projects, Practice	GMC Publications	Useful Woodturning Projects	GMC Publications
Green Woodwork	Mike Abbott	Woodturning: A Foundation Course	Keith Rowley
Illustrated Woodturning Techniques	John Hunnex	Woodturning Jewellery	Hilary Bowen
Keith Rowley's Woodturning Projects	Keith Rowley	Woodturning Masterclass	Tony Boase
Make Money from Woodturning	Ann & Bob Phillips	Woodturning: A Source Book of Shapes	John Hunnex
Multi-Centre Woodturning	Ray Hopper	Woodturning Techniques	GMC Publications
		Woodturning Wizardry	David Springett

WOODCARVING

The Art of the Woodcarver	GMC Publications	Wildfowl Carving Volume 1	Jim Pearce
Carving Birds & Beasts	GMC Publications	Wildfowl Carving Volume 2	Jim Pearce
Carving Realistic Birds	David Tippey	Woodcarving: A Complete Course	Ron Butterfield
Carving on Turning	Chris Pye	Woodcarving for Beginners: Projects, Techniques & Tools	
Decorative Woodcarving	Jeremy Williams		GMC Publications
Practical Tips for Turners & Carvers	GMC Publications	Woodcarving Tools, Materials & Equipment	Chris Pye

PLANS, PROJECTS, TOOLS & THE WORKSHOP

40 More Woodworking Plans & Projects	GMC Publications	Sharpening: The Complete Guide	Jim Kingshott
Electric Woodwork: Power Tool Woodworking	Jeremy Broun	Sharpening Pocket Reference Book	Jim Kingshott
The Incredible Router	Jeremy Broun	Woodworking Plans & Projects	GMC Publications
Making & Modifying Woodworking Tools	Jim Kingshott	The Workshop	Jim Kingshott

TOYS & MINIATURES

Designing & Making Wooden Toys	Terry Kelly	Making Wooden Toys & Games	Jeff & Jennie Loader
Heraldic Miniature Knights	Peter Greenhill	Miniature Needlepoint Carpets	Janet Granger
Making Board, Peg & Dice Games	Jeff & Jennie Loader	Restoring Rocking Horses	Clive Green & Anthony Dew
Making Little Boxes from Wood	John Bennett	Turning Miniatures in Wood	John Sainsbury
Making Unusual Miniatures	Graham Spalding	Turning Wooden Toys	Terry Lawrence

CREATIVE CRAFTS

The Complete Pyrography	Stephen Poole	Creating Knitwear Designs	Pat Ashforth & Steve Plummer
Cross Stitch on Colour	Sheena Rogers	Making Knitwear Fit	Pat Ashforth & Steve Plummer
Embroidery Tips & Hints	Harold Hayes	Miniature Needlepoint Carpets	Janet Granger
		Tatting Collage: Adventurous Ideas for Tatters	Lindsay Rogers

UPHOLSTERY AND FURNITURE

Care & Repair	*GMC Publications*	Making Shaker Furniture	*Barry Jackson*
Complete Woodfinishing	*Ian Hosker*	Seat Weaving (Practical Crafts)	*Ricky Holdstock*
Furniture Projects	*Rod Wales*	Upholsterer's Pocket Reference Book	*David James*
Furniture Restoration (Practical Crafts)	*Kevin Jan Bonner*	Upholstery: A Complete Course	*David James*
Furniture Restoration & Repair for Beginners	*Kevin Jan Bonner*	Upholstery: Techniques & Projects	*David James*
Green Woodwork	*Mike Abbott*	Woodfinishing Handbook (Practical Crafts)	*Ian Hosker*
Making Fine Furniture	*Tom Darby*		

DOLLS' HOUSES & DOLLS' HOUSE FURNITURE

Architecture for Dolls' Houses	*Joyce Percival*	Making Period Dolls' House Accessories	*Andrea Barham*
The Complete Dolls' House Book	*Jean Nisbett*	Making Period Dolls' House Furniture	*Derek & Sheila Rowbottom*
Easy-to-Make Dolls' House Accessories	*Andrea Barham*	Making Tudor Dolls' Houses	*Derek Rowbottom*
Make Your Own Dolls' House Furniture	*Maurice Harper*	Making Victorian Dolls' House Furniture	*Patricia King*
Making Dolls' House Furniture	*Patricia King*	Miniature Needlepoint Carpets	*Janet Granger*
Making Georgian Dolls' Houses	*Derek Rowbottom*	The Secrets of the Dolls' House Makers	*Jean Nisbett*

OTHER BOOKS

Guide to Marketing	*GMC Publications*	Woodworkers' Career & Educational Source Book	*GMC Publications*

VIDEOS

Carving a Figure: The Female Form	*Ray Gonzalez*	Elliptical Turning	*David Springett*
The Traditional Upholstery Workshop		Woodturning Wizardry	*David Springett*
Part 1: *Drop-in & Pinstuffed Seats*	*David James*	Turning Between Centres: The Basics	*Dennis White*
The Traditional Upholstery Workshop		Turning Bowls	*Dennis White*
Part 2: *Stuffover Upholstery*	*David James*	Boxes, Goblets & Screw Threads	*Dennis White*
Hollow Turning	*John Jordan*	Novelties & Projects	*Dennis White*
Bowl Turning	*John Jordan*	Classic Profiles	*Dennis White*
Sharpening Turning & Carving Tools	*Jim Kingshott*	Twists & Advanced Turning	*Dennis White*
Sharpening the Professional Way	*Jim Kingshott*		

MAGAZINES

WOODTURNING ● WOODCARVING ● BUSINESSMATTERS

The above represents a full list of all titles currently published or scheduled to be published. All are available direct from the Publishers or through bookshops, newsagents and specialist retailers. To place an order, or to obtain a complete catalogue, contact:

GMC Publications, 166 High Street, Lewes, East Sussex BN7 1XU United Kingdom
Tel: 01273 488005 Fax: 01273 478606

Orders by credit card are accepted